# ...ISE FOR
## MORE SALES PLEASE

*More Sales Please* is the ultimate companion for any small business owner who is looking to be seen and make their voice heard, break down the seemingly 'dark art' of social media and connect with more customers to make sales. This is a 'must have' in the toolkit of any founder, full of wisdom, insight and practical advice, distilled into one, brilliant book.

**Holly Tucker MBE, Founder of notonthehighstreet and Holly & Co**

Hooray – this book is written with small business owners in mind! *More Sales Please* is packed with tips, actions and inspiration to show you how to make sales with ease. If you find selling and promoting awkward, if you are looking to increase sales without increasing your workload, or if you're looking for a resource filled with straightforward advice that will help your business grow, this is the book for you.

**Emma Jones CBE, Founder of Enterprise Nation**

When women learn to sell, amazing things happen. *More Sales Please* will teach you how.

**Lauren Currie, Founder of Upfront**

Sara is the ultimate champion. Through her warmth and encouragement she's empowered thousands of us to have the courage to show up and be seen. And through sharing her knowledge and incredible proven experience she's giving us the power to make real change happen for ourselves and our businesses. I dare you to read this book and not make more sales – you couldn't have a better guide!

**Lucy Sheridan, The Comparison Coach**

In an online business world flooded with sales gimmicks, hacks and quick fixes, this book stands out as a beacon of authenticity, longevity and integrity. Sara masterfully and empathetically challenges the stereotypes of selling, urging us to embrace a sales approach grounded in genuine communication, strong ethics and transparency.

The candid anecdotes, compelling arguments, practical activities and expert tips make this book a sales toolkit. Sara not only demystifies the art of selling but also empowers business owners to promote themselves with confidence. *More Sales Please* is a must-read for anyone who wants to merge profit with purpose in the modern business landscape.

**Tamu Thomas, Life and Business Coach**

*More Sales Please* will forever change how you approach selling, how you feel about selling AND give you the kick-up-the-bum you need to start seeing results! Everyone needs Sara in their business life. She's so freakin' knowledgeable, and everything she shares comes from a genuine desire for you to succeed in your business. Not only that, but she also empowers you to take action, to realise that you CAN show up, talk about your offers and MAKE SALES!

**Steph Caswell, Founder of Creating Happy Writers**

This book is a refreshing sales read that cuts through the slime and ick of bro selling strategies. If you want tangible and practical advice to not only give you confidence to sell but actually feel energized and excited by it, this is a must-read.

**Lucy Werner, Founder of Hype Yourself**

This is a book I wish I had read ten years ago. As women we've been taught to play small, be grateful for what we have and to not to ask for more. But Sara tears up that narrative. *More Sales Please* does exactly what it says on the tin: it's easy to read, it's stuffed full of actionable advice and it's a total game changer for anyone who is struggling with the idea of making more money or winging it with selling. Sara is the trusted expert and friend everyone needs. Run, don't walk to read this book – devour it from cover to cover, and watch your confidence, your opportunities and your income soar.

**Lara Sheldrake, Founder, Found and Flourish**

Every small business owner leading with integrity should read this book. Sara is the business expert you wish you knew in real life. Knowledgeable, infectious and full of expertise on how to get your products selling well from day one. Thankfully, she's written *More Sales Please* so now we have her on hand whenever we need her! A goldmine of easy to implement tips and action steps that will show you how to increase your sales without sleaze.

**Vix Meldrew, Online Learning Expert**

Sara has an extremely rare talent for simplifying the mystifying art of selling without the ick, and this book is both a must-read masterpiece, and a must-devour masterclass in ethical, efficient and effective selling online. Read this book, and your bank account will thank you for it.

**Kerry Lyons, Creative Coach and Illustrator**

Finally! A guide to sales for small business that teaches you how to quickly master the basics with confidence and ease.

**Liana Fricker, Founder of The Inspiration Space**

Selling is a word that often fills business owners with fear. But Sara has managed to turn it into a manageable process that doesn't feel icky. If you want to increase your visibility and show up in a way that feels authentic to you, this is a must read.

**Rosie Davies-Smith, Founder of PR Dispatch**

I struggle to read books these days but I POURED over this one. The way Sara breaks down everyday selling is practical, achievable and (most importantly) fun! The real-life examples are so helpful and the activities mean you can implement the teachings as you go along. I'd recommend this book to anyone struggling to consistently sell online, or IRL. I will definitely be applying Sara's teachings to my own business and can't wait to see the results!

**Amanda Perry, ADHD Business Coach and Strategist**

Finally, a book on selling that is honest, practical and hugely inspiring! I've been waiting for someone to write a book just like this and I'm so happy it was Sara who did! Her no ick, no nonsense, no shame approach to sales is exactly what we all need. This book will make you more money! It really is that simple.

**Ray Dodd, Money and Business Coach**

SARA NASSER DALRYMPLE

# MORE SALES PLEASE

**Promote your small business online**

Make consistent sales

**Grow without the grind**

First published in Great Britain by Practical Inspiration Publishing, 2024

ISBN   9781788604659 (PB Print)
          9781788605755 (HB Print)
          9781788604673 (epub)
          9781788604666 (mobi)

Want to bulk-buy copies of this book for your team and colleagues? We can customize the content and co-brand *More Sales Please* to suit your business's needs.

Please email info@practicalinspiration.com for more details.

Practical Inspiration
Publishing

# Dedication

To all the purpose-driven small business owners who have taken the leap to realise their dream, and sure as heck aren't going to compromise their ethics to get there. This one's for you.

# Contents

# Introduction

When I was 32, I started my working life from scratch. Taking the leap from banker to business owner was liberating *and* the polar opposite of The Plan. It was also totally terrifying, because I hadn't the foggiest idea what I was doing.

There are so many reasons why people set up their own businesses – family, freedom, flexibility over their time. For me it was all three, and if figuring out how to be my own boss was what was needed, well, that was what I was going to do.

Ten years in banking taught me how to hit seven-figure targets handed to me from up high. I was good at doing as I was told, which was to set my alarm for 6 am, wedge myself onto a hot and sweaty central line train in rush hour and be at my desk for 7.30 am to make it happen (whatever 'it' was). I knew how to turn existing relationships into sales. I knew how to be a good employee. I knew how to make money for the corporate machine.

What I didn't know how to do was make money for myself, on my own. Put myself out there. Get a website. Tell people I existed and was Open For Business. I had no clue how to use social media, let alone *talk* on it, and frankly, the whole concept was beyond overwhelming. Nobody in my family has their own business. In my life thus far, I'd been the person always ducking out of speaking in front of big groups or being in front of any kind of camera whatsoever. My voice would go all wobbly when I had to do presentations. I should also mention I'm one of the least techy people around.

Being a business owner was a whole new world and it required a whole new skillset. I took my quivering voice and my camera shyness and my distinct lack of entrepreneurial background and I found a way to build a business I love anyway. I feel qualified to say, if I can do it, you can absolutely do it, too.

Since then, I've taught hundreds of other business owners how to get visible, feel camera confident, and, for the past few years, increase the sales in their own businesses. I've found my happy place helping small businesses with the sales skills they need to survive long term, and I'm so glad you're here because now I'm going to help you, too.

## Why I wrote this book

*Nothing happens in business until someone sells something.*

(Henry Ford)

Let's be real: money is needed to fuel your business and your main source of money is sales. In fact, until clients are flowing in regularly, until you're making more money than you're spending, and until you're confident in your ability to keep bringing in buyers month in, month out, your business is on somewhat shaky ground.

So many business owners are held back by a fear of selling. Twenty per cent of businesses fail in the first year and 60% in the first three years.[1] Of these, over half cited running out of money or being outcompeted as reasons for failing. That fear of selling will ultimately contribute to many more of those businesses failing than otherwise would.

The vast majority of new business owners have had no prior sales training, do not have a plan when it comes to how they'll make sales, and are starting out with very little confidence in their ability to sell well.

Six out of ten of the country's small businesses don't use social media to promote themselves and almost half said they could have made more sales if they had marketed themselves

---

[1] https://fundsquire.co.uk/startup-statistics/ and www.nerdwallet.com/uk/business/start-up-failure-statistics/

properly online, according to a recent poll.[2] Having no online presence is a big risk to visibility, sales and revenue. Having an online presence but not knowing how to make it work, is equally problematic. Recent data obtained by small business advice and inspiration hub Holly & Co revealed 92% of small businesses don't feel seen, heard or loved online.[3] No matter what type of business you have, the strength of your ability to promote what you do and make sales plays a fundamental role in whether it's a long-term success or not.

It's not nearly as hard as you think to build a business filled with happy clients, consistent sales and a stable income. This book centres around the following key themes:

1. Sales confidence is a huge gap for business owners which stops thousands getting visible. Small, repeatable actions to promote what you do are how we close that gap.

2. If every business owner spent just a few minutes promoting what they do each day, more sales would be made and the combined impact on the economy would be huge.

3. The magic of social media to promote your business via the method in this book is that it's quick, it's effective and it won't burn you out.

Anyone – yes anyone – can learn how to sell well, and everyone – yes everyone - that does so benefits financially from having that skill. This is your guide to feeling confident in your ability to sell anything, at any price point, in a way that's natural, automatic and gets results. It will show you how to feel clear, confident and at ease with the way you bring in buyers.

---

[2] www.independent.co.uk/news/business/uk-businesses-social-media-poll-b1852747.html
[3] https://holly.co/campaign-shop-independent-2023/

# Small business, big impact

Small businesses are a *big deal*. There are over 5.5 million small businesses in the UK,[4] and together they generate a quarter of the country's GDP. Over half of the private sector's turnover comes from small and medium sized enterprises (SMEs). Recent data show that SMEs in the UK created a combined turnover of more than £2.18 trillion in 2022, which amounts to over half of the private sector's overall turnover.[5]

According to a recent study looking at female entrepreneurship in the UK, it is estimated that an additional £250 billion of new value could be added to the UK economy if women started and scaled new businesses at the same rate as men.[6] To add to this, if trillions of pounds are made even with 60% not taking advantage of the benefits of promoting online, imagine how much additional income could be generated if more small business owners knew how to confidently promote their businesses and sell.

To say the small business community is crucial for the UK economy is an understatement, and it's essential for long-term economic growth that the small business community continues to thrive.

*The small business community IS the UK economy.*

My belief is that the more business owners equip themselves with solid sales skills, the more impact we will make. When you are confident in your sales skills, you'll always be able to make money and you'll do it with more ease. This doesn't only benefit you, it also positively impacts your family, your community and the economy as a whole.

---

[4] https://startups.co.uk/analysis/small-business-statistics/ and www.capital ontap.com/en/blog/posts/small-business-big-impact-the-contribution-of-small-businesses-to-the-uk-economy/

[5] www.statista.com/statistics/687367/uk-sme-turnover/

[6] https://assets.publishing.service.gov.uk/government/uploads/system/uploads/attachment_data/file/784324/RoseReview_Digital_FINAL.PDF

# Who the book is for

If you're looking for sleazy sales methods, this isn't the book for you. There won't be any tactics or hard selling here. We'll focus instead on how to confidently present the information your buyer craves and that helps them make decisions that are right for them, all in their own sweet time. Zero force. Zilch push. Zip ick.

You *are* in the right place if:

- You are craving a more reliable flow to sales and income but you don't want to rely on complicated launches, funnels or anything that feels like a 'tactic' to get there.
- When it comes to sales, marketing and showing up online it feels like you're guessing at the right actions to take. You want someone to understand your options and feel clear about the right next steps for you to increase sales.
- You're ready for sales to happen comfortably, but consistently. No sleaze, no exhausting systems, just brilliant experiences your clients won't be able to stop raving about.

# How to use this book

I've distilled your roadmap to selling well into ten chapters, each one devoted to a key sales activity that will ensure the way you show up is effective, easy and fun. Every chapter is a deep dive into that essential action and includes inspiring stories and expert tips from business owners who have journeyed to find their ease with selling. You'll find the key non-negotiable action for each chapter labelled 'VIP' (very important point) with activities to help you take action as you go.

The book is split into three parts, as follows:

Part I brings clarity to why selling feels so uncomfortable to so many, and what you can do about it. So much of what we think about selling is the result of bad role modelling, big business practices and a general lack of understanding about what it means to sell well. You'll discover exactly what your non-negotiable actions are, where to focus your time, and how to create a whole new standard of selling. This is so that you feel clearer about what to do and why to do it, and to free you from the idea that you have to do it anyone else's way. Goodbye trepidation, hello new found enthusiasm!

Part II boosts your confidence by walking you through the foundations of integrity-led selling. When you have a plan, you feel more confident and when you feel more confident, it's easier to show up and be seen. Being visible has so many benefits for sales. It connects you with more ideal clients. It builds your brand awareness, so that people know who you are and how you help. It establishes your credibility and expertise. It makes the whole sales process easier. You'll discover what to do, the order to do it in and how to make sure everything aligns to your personality.

In Part III you'll gain new levels of ease in promoting your products using social media to superspeed results. Everything you need to show up as yourself and set your wheels in motion is right here. Being a small business owner in the digital age presents an *enormous* opportunity, and everything in this part exists to help you increase your consistency with promoting so that you can take full advantage of that.

This book will help you take daily sales action in a way that feels natural and effortless to you. By the end you'll have everything you need to confidently promote your products online with ease and make consistent sales. Use it to make sure you are showing up for your business in a way that makes you money and is highly effective. The intention is to equip you with the sales skills you need to save you time, save you heartache, and save your business from going under.

So, what are we waiting for? Let's get going!

# Part I

# More sales clarity

When it comes to being seen and increasing sales, not knowing what to do has a really big impact on the small business economy. It's impossible to quantify the big-ness exactly, but when you consider the fact that over 90% said they felt invisible in a recent poll conducted by Holly & Co, it's *big*.

I want you to get to your destination (consistent sales!) as quickly as possible. Everyone starts from a different place, bringing different experiences and thoughts about what it means to sell. Knowing where you're starting your adventure with sales will help you understand what's holding you back. Let's kick things off with some basic truths and untruths and get crystal clear on the key activities that create sales: your 'non-negotiables' of selling well.

In Parts II and III you'll get into the practical action required for consistent sales. Part I is all about having the information you need to create a sales plan you can not only get behind, but stay behind. These first four chapters will give you the clarity you need to get started and save you time later on.

When your sales process is solid and you know how to bring in clients, there are so many things you don't need to waste your time worrying about. You don't need a massive audience, you don't need to seek out tonnes of PR opportunities, you don't even need to be online for more than a few minutes per day. Wherever you're at on your sales journey, if you want more buyers, this part will show you what to focus your time and energy on.

Highlighter pen at the ready – it all starts here!

# Chapter 1

# So, this is sales

*I bring fresh flowers to every event because I want everyone to feel special.*

(Lara Sheldrake, community building expert)

When I first started promoting my business on social media, it felt like I'd landed on Mars. I knew how to sell and market in the 'real' world, but all of a sudden, I was a newbie again. I didn't have a clue about how to use Instagram for business, or how to create sales opportunities there. It felt like my very first day in a new job, where you don't know where the loos are, and you spend all day trying to smile and fit in.

The place was awash with 'rules' specific to online business. It seemed like I'd walked through a door into a new land – one with a whole new language I needed to learn how to speak, full of words I'd never heard before, like algorithm and discovery calls and memes and hashtags. This was back in the times when Instagram for me had been a photo sharing app, nothing more. The step-up to using it as a sales tool felt huge. It was overwhelming.

Everybody seemed to be saying something different about what was required to have success and find clients online, and as a brand new business owner I was caught like a rabbit in the headlights. I knew I wanted to make social media work for me, but *how?*

The answer was long and multifaceted:
'You need to grow your audience to 10,000 followers first!'
'You need a lead magnet!'
'You need a clear niche and to be known for one thing!'
'You need a Facebook group!'
'You need to go live every day!'
'You need to handle objections!'
Oof.

What a huge amount to navigate. Social media was (still is) awash with 'guru'-style online coaches proclaiming to have the must-have systems and strategies that every business *needs* to have in place. Quick-fixes, fancy hacks and must-have scripts – it was all there and it was all shiny and waving its jazzhands at me. So, I did what I've always been taught to do when approaching something new: I rolled up my sleeves to immerse myself in learning.

All I needed to do, it seemed, was invest in all of the courses, learn all of the things, and I'd be off! My keenness to learn led me down a path of spending well over £10,000 on courses and programmes in online business. I spent almost all of it being taught the online version of how to sell, how to market, and how to connect people with the services I wanted to offer.

*If you're scratching your head thinking, 'Hang on Sara, don't you have a background in sales, didn't you work in corporate sales for years, isn't selling exactly what your previous ten-year career taught you how to do?'* then you'd be spot on. But as a newbie business owner on the scene, I didn't want to take a 'wrong turn'. I didn't want to waste time doing things that weren't going to work online, and if there was a special set of rules, I absolutely wanted to know what they were.

If I can save you some of the time I spent in various rabbit holes working out what is versus what is not required when it comes to promoting your business online, so that you can build your marketing and sales plan around what feels good to you, I'll be thrilled. Before we gallop ahead though, let's get on the same page with what selling actually means/does not mean.

# What is selling?

The *Cambridge Dictionary* defines selling and sales as:

*Selling: the activity of making products and services available so that people buy them.*

*Sales: the number of items sold.*[1]

To me that says, put your products and services out into the world in such a way that (a) they'll be seen by people and (b) those people will want to buy them.

One of the great things about being a business owner is that you are now responsible for the income you make. Exciting, right? Your ability to pay yourself well and sustain yourself financially is dependent on your ability to do these activities well, consistently, and in a way that feels effortless to you. The number of items you sell each month is the result of the quality of your selling activities in the weeks and months preceding that month. It all makes sense.

# Sales skills

If sales are the lifeblood of your business, then sales skills are the foundation from which you make money. They are the engine of your business and how you connect people to how your products and services can help them. The way you communicate the specific value of what you do has the power to make it easy for people looking for that exact thing to feel the pull to work with you. The better you feel when talking about your products, the more your clients will see you not just as someone they want to buy from, but someone they are excited and enthusiastic to work with. Sales skills ensure you position yourself as the only option worth choosing.

A business without solid sales skills is like a house built on mud. It might look OK from the outside, to begin with the

---

[1] https://dictionary.cambridge.org/dictionary/english/sell

kerb appeal could even be outstanding, but longer term, if it's built on uneven ground or doesn't have the concrete foundations to keep it up, it will simply fall apart. Without firm sales skills, growing a business that's profitable can feel like a slow and painful waiting game. It's not easy to secure a steady stream of incoming clients if you're unclear about what to say or how to get noticed by the people you want to work with.

Solid sales skills enable you to:

- make money from day one;
- become profitable as quickly as possible;
- build a business that lasts long term;
- work effectively and efficiently so the business doesn't drain all your time;
- ensure your clients have the information they need to make easy decisions.

Sales skills are not a 'nice to have' – they are absolutely essential when you have your own business. Without them, your ability to make money will always be limited to only the very few people who can find you on their own, and already know they want what you're selling, without any involvement from you whatsoever. That's not enough to sustain a business.

---

**Just a few of the things you can rely on your sales skills to help with:**

1. Signing your first client – and your hundredth!
2. Promoting your business online.
3. Making sure the people who work with you feel delighted with their experience.
4. Negotiating with team members.
5. Putting powerful proposals together.
6. Attracting invitations to be on podcasts and speak on stages.
7. Deciding how to show up.
8. Securing investment for your business.

# Marketing and selling: aren't they the same thing?

The *Cambridge Dictionary* defines marketing as:

> *Marketing: a job that involves encouraging people to buy a product or service.*[2]

To me, that says the two go hand in hand when you're a small business owner.

In a corporate setting, marketing teams and sales teams are often separate. This was certainly the case in my corporate days. In big businesses, there are whole teams of people devoted to marketing and designing promotional materials for relationship managers to use, before passing clients to the sales teams to 'close the deal'. At the sales desk I worked on, we had often not actually met our clients, because the relationship was managed elsewhere. Our job was simply to convert an existing relationship into a sale.

This is important to note, because all sales start with a relationship. In corporate settings it is managed elsewhere, but in small business it's different. Whether you are a product- or a service-based business, your relationship with your client *is* personal. It is of utmost importance that your client gets to know *you*, as well as your services, well before they buy from you. As such, as a small business owner, marketing and selling are inextricably intertwined. Each has an equal role to play in the sales process. As the sole promoter/marketer of your business, the role of your sales and marketing activities is to help your audience make decisions. One won't work without the other: you need them both.

If you only have marketing but no selling, you can spend as much time as you like creating content, but none of it will convert to a sale because the client never reaches a decision.

---

[2] https://dictionary.cambridge.org/dictionary/english/marketing

If you only spend your time selling, you will miss out the crucial stages of building relationships, providing context and nurturing your audience, which set you up for sales success. Either in isolation causes your endeavours to fall flat. Both are required, and therefore the rest of this book will focus on the sales process: that is, your sales and marketing activity combined, as one entity.

Marketing can often incorporate more of the higher level, business-specific messaging: for example, the way you talk about 'what you do' when you're at a networking event or the elevator pitch that you use. It gives people the initial information about your business, why it exists, and the type of work that you do, but it doesn't necessarily take people into the specifics required or far enough into the process for a sale to be made.

Selling is the messaging that you use when you're helping potential clients get to know or understand your products and services or a specific way that you work. It's the part of the process that helps people arrive at the ability to make a decision on that individual product. Both are absolutely required in the sales process, and work in tandem much of the time.

## What is the sales process?

For the avoidance of any doubt, in this book the sales process refers to the set of predefined actions that you deem necessary to help potential clients arrive at a place where they are equipped and informed to make an empowered decision about whether or not to buy from you. It exists to bring as much clarity as possible to your audience about what working with you or buying from you will be like.

Typically, this involves a combination of steps incorporating marketing and selling actions (building connections and forming relationships, lead generation, listening to needs, nurturing your audience and offering solutions that are tailored to that need).

Your sales process forms a nice, neat pathway to a sale. It will be different for each individual business, according to preference, personality and the potential clients you are calling in. It is the journey to either a yes or a no, and incorporates everything that happens to aid the decision maker make the right decision for them (no matter the outcome for you).

Trying to achieve regular sales without a robust plan is like being on a rollercoaster you can't get off. Your sales skills, process, client service and promotional activity are the building blocks that allow you to create consistent sales with an experience your clients love as much as you do. Understanding the steps involved helps you to create a process that is efficient, effective and builds enthusiasm with your clients.

Knowing your non-negotiable activities – your needle movers – stops you trying everything everywhere all at once, only to later discover 99% of that effort wasn't right for your business anyway. Exhausting. The role of the sales process is to generate revenue, to grow your business and to keep you sane.

## Feel-good selling

*I've learned that people will forget what you said, people will forget what you did, but people will never forget how you made them feel.*

(Maya Angelou)

Having a process that's well thought-out and considered is way more than a means to an end. It also creates a high-quality experience for clients, who will interact with your business many times before they buy.

Your sales process has the power to stop someone in their tracks and instantly make them feel seen, heard, excited and intrigued. Or, if the process isn't doing its job properly, like something rather unpleasant you've just found on the bottom of your shoe. Which way that goes is everything to do with how focused you are on creating not just a sale, but an experience that starts long before anyone pays you. I am very big on the power of a high-quality experience, and I hope by the end of this book (if not chapter!) you will be, too. Creating an experience you genuinely love makes selling it a lot easier and helps your buyer enjoy the process more, too. Sales is an exchange of energy, and I don't know about you but I want people to buy from me from a happy, excited place, not under duress. Being experience focused sets you apart, it allows people to feel excited, and it gets you a reputation as someone who cares. And that's *really* good for business.

For decades the standard of the seller–purchaser encounter has been – varied – to say the least. Shoddy practices and sleazy stereotypes have a lot to answer for as you'll see in Chapter 2. So, before we go any further, I want to invite you to set a new standard. One where integrity and the client experience stays front and centre. One that's effective because its focus isn't on you, but on doing all you can to ensure your client is able to make a decision that feels right for them. From now on, the focus is to make selling less about you, and more about your client and how you can enable them to reach their buying decision with ease, at the right time for them.

A good sales experience stays with you because it *feels* amazing. If you want to be memorable, focus on how you'll make your client feel – even before they are paying you. It's the difference between buying from someone once, and buying again and again, even when it means travelling, waiting longer to be seen or spending more than other options available and telling all your pals. We all have tonnes of really excellent buying experiences to draw on. So, let's also examine the good, and not just the bad.

As small business owners we have more licence than big business to make every buying experience personal and memorable. We do not hand our clients over to different departments for separate stages in the journey – we have the ability to provide consistency of care that larger companies cannot. A sales experience transcends the period of time before you buy, what you bought itself and what happens after the experience is over. All three phases are important because if something is missing from any one of them, as buyers we remember it.

If selling feels in any way awkward to you right now, my first recommendation is that you shift focus towards the overall experience your potential clients are having. When you focus on the overall experience people have when they interact with your business, you put your client first, and then your sales activity becomes part of that commitment – how can you not show up for people when you know their overall experience will be better when you do? It's a clever mindset shift that is small but also mighty, and it never fails.

 Sales is an exchange of energy. It feels good to create and sell something you genuinely love, so let's make that the new standard.

## Lara Sheldrake on ... selling what you love

Lara Sheldrake is a community expert and the creator of a business network for women and non-binary people called Found and Flourish, which has hosted over 250 events since 2019. Her business exists to educate, connect and inspire founders and freelancers and she believes that community and kindness are key ingredients to creating the right kind of environment for people to flourish.

There's a reason Lara is regularly asked to speak on panels, podcasts and in the press and has over 15,000 people following her on Instagram, and her genuine passion for community is it. It's clear from the first moment you land on the Found and Flourish Instagram page that this is a place to feel included, close the opportunity gap and create shared success through the power of the collective experience. So it's no wonder that every time she runs one of her wildly successful 'Hugs and Brunch' in-person events, it sells out in two shakes of a lamb's tail. Her audience already know how warm, nurturing and supportive the events will be long before they attend one, because they've already seen these qualities running throughout each and every interaction they have had with her up to that point.

By putting such a strong focus on equality and inclusion, Lara has created a loyal legion of fans who know exactly what she stands for – and importantly – they've already experienced it. This allows people to buy with confidence and enthusiasm, and they do – again and again. (I should know, I'm one of them!)

I asked Lara to reflect on how she's grown Hugs and Brunch to be such a well-loved part of her business over the past few years and to share her wisdom on creating an experience that has such a loyal client base. Here's what she said:

'Running a business shouldn't have to be lonely – and yet that's exactly how I felt before I started Found and Flourish.

I have never enjoyed networking events – they never felt like "me". I used to struggle to find the energy to go to them and whenever I did, I always left feeling like there was something missing – something magic, vulnerable and fun. I often felt lonely as a business owner and wanted that to change.

I set up Found and Flourish to do something about it and incorporated hugs, connection and collaboration into our brunches which gave the events a warm, relaxed feel. It felt refreshing, and liberating, to network in this way. It's a safe and welcoming space where nobody needs to be worried about not knowing anyone.

Everyone leaves feeling inspired, connected and less lonely. And, of course, if they've won a new client in the process it's the cherry on the cake.

Some online purchasing experiences can be very cold and transactional. I want our experience to feel the opposite: like you're straight away speaking with or meeting up with old friends or that you're opening up an email from someone you feel you've known forever. Trust, authenticity and kindness are important to me.

My events are personal, light and inspiring and people feel so comfortable they forget they're there to talk about business. In fact, people rarely chat business and end up opening up in a way they've never opened up before. Their words, not mine! And this is where the magic of true relationship building happens. I bring fresh flowers to each event and personal touches to dress the table with because I want everyone to feel special.'

 **Lara's top tips**

Build a know, like, trust relationship with your audience. Share your values often, be clear about why you're doing what you do and consistently show up in a way that people start to associate you with the thing you're passionate about most. This has helped me create a well-loved experience that people want to share with others. Ensuring everyone feels comfortable and inspired means attendees want to tell others about how they were made to feel. A feeling of consistency is important too: my members know what to expect every time.

Find Lara on Instagram @lara_sheldrake or join her Found and Flourish community @foundflourish or at www.foundflourish.com and feel immediately at ease.

# Now it's your turn!

## To create and sell something you love

Think of the best sales experience you've ever had. What did you like about it? Was it the way you were spoken to, was it the clarity of the process and the way you were kept informed of what each next step would be? Was it an overall energy or feeling that you had? Or something else?

What are the hallmarks for you of a good sales experience? This could be the level of personalization, feeling listened to and understood, simplicity of making your purchase, how you felt, or something else! Starting to jot down ideas of what you like in the sales experience will help you frame how you do things in your business.

Now think about the worst. What didn't you like about it? Was it the way you were spoken to, was it to do with the process? Was it an overall energy or feeling that you had? Or something else? What do you wish had been different?

Taking your personal experiences above into account, think about what kind of experience you want to create for your clients, whether they are brand new into your world or returning to work with you for the tenth time? What is non-negotiable for you that your prospective clients experience in your sales process? This could be tangible, a feeling, or something else! You get to choose, so make it excellent!

# Chapter recap

- Marketing and selling are both part of the sales process when you're a small business owner, they cannot be separated.
- If you're not a fan of rollercoasters, waiting ages for anything to happen or leaving the number of clients you have to chance, have a well thought-out sales process, and stick to it!

- As a small business owner you have the ability to create the exact experience you want your clients to have, even before they pay you. This helps you stand out with ideal clients who value integrity as much as you do.
- Sell what you love, it feels really good.

OK, that's some basics handled. Now we know what we're aiming for, let's dive into some common myths about selling and look at how much they can hold you back (often without you even realizing).

# Chapter 2

# Ditch the myths

*The ick is a lie: selling is just telling people about your great product.*

(Helen Perry, marketing whizz)

Have you ever felt like you are the only business owner in the world who *isn't* selling out programmes, growing at the speed of light and setting off celebratory confetti cannons all over social media to mark how easy it all is?

When you're showing up, trying with all your might and devoting more of yourself to your business than you ever expected to, but still not yet seeing the traction you'd like, it can leave you feeling exhausted, burned out and quite frankly, fed up. For most people it takes time, patience, planning and perseverance to grow a business that stands the test of time. If you're looking for a quick fix, one-size-fits-all strategy for a million dollar business in two minutes flat, this isn't the book for you.

I'm on a mission to empower you to feel good about the way you sell and to do it in a way that's really natural, effortless and to everyone's benefit. I like to keep things simple and always in keeping with your personality, values and your current stage of business.

So do you know what really grinds my gears? People selling substandard products and spewing out empty promises. It makes the rest of us look bad when, in reality, the vast majority of small business owners are here to do good and help people. The elephant in the room is: why is the standard of selling in the online space often so... crud? 'Follow my winning strategy, the golden rule of selling is always be closing, never ever do this, buy this script, use this fail-safe template, don't sell anything until you've grown a mahoosive audience…'

I've seen it all.

Along life's rich tapestry I've been promised '1:1 calls and support at every step' only to make my investment and never hear from the coach again. I've been encouraged to buy things within a certain time limit to access additional bonuses that have never materialized. I've invested with coaches who have purported to get to know their clients and their businesses, only to discover that six months later, they still didn't even know my name – let alone what my business was up to.

I bet you know what I'm talking about. It goes on far too much and it would be remiss of me not to acknowledge that. I strongly suspect we have all had a nasty sales experience at some point or another. So if you're nodding along, I really sympathize. But don't let that silence you or make you fear showing up in an altogether more authentic way.

Salespeople are often portrayed as greedy, untrustworthy con artists who are only out for themselves, and, unfortunately, that stereotype is sometimes true. But this is not the whole picture by any means. It is nothing at all like the caring, creative, community-focused business owners I work with every day. The world needs more integrity-led sellers to even out the situation. How does the industry change if the dominant players are still pumping out this 'guru knows best and it's my way or the highway' approach to growing a business online?

Strong, purpose-driven brands are typically based on passion and a deep desire to help people, not to rip them off! In fact, what I've found to be true more often than I'd like to see in the creative communities is that people are so keen to help that they're often working for free or doing it for such a small fee that they can't cover their bills. Fear around selling is so expensive for the small business economy. It leads many business owners to be so afraid of looking 'pushy' that they would rather not ask to be paid for their work at all!

Lots of small businesses aren't participating as fully in selling as they should be, which affects their growth, not to mention their margins. According to a recent study, six out of ten small business owners don't use social media to promote their business, and 40% are completely unaware of how to do it.[1]

Sales stereotypes are harmful because they stop you participating and impact the money you make. And that has a knock-on effect on the economy as a whole. The number one job of your business is to get you paid for work you love to do. Not to give it all away for free! Imagine the huge difference that could be made if more businesses participated in actively promoting their products.

Getting visible to sell with confidence, making money *and* having integrity. Yes please.

Creating a business and not allowing people to buy from you is a bit like creating a delicious dinner banquet and then not actually inviting anyone round to enjoy it, so after slaving away at a hot stove all day you watch your culinary creations go straight in the bin. What a waste of all that time and care and effort.

In the next chapter you'll diagnose your specific sales problem, but for now let me just say that you – a business owner with integrity by the boatload – not selling doesn't do anything whatsoever to change the dominant narrative. Offering things for free because it feels less 'icky', whether that is social media content, emails, or free audits that help people, is only helpful to your audience if, at some point, you also sell to them and tell them what they can do next. Hoarding your prowess helps nobody – you have to invite people to buy from you in order for real change to be made.

I have seen *so* many myths and just plain lies about what selling involves or should look like over the years. A lot of them

---

[1] www.independent.co.uk/news/business/uk-businesses-social-media-poll-b1852747.html

stem from outdated methods or selling in big business, neither of which are useful reference points to online business owners like you and me.

Let's delve into some fundamental myths about what sales is and how selling works so that we can squash them into oblivion and create a new (vastly more palatable) narrative.

## Myth 1: Selling is icky, manipulative, sleazy or pushy

This myth incorporates the belief that selling is about tricking your client into buying something they don't want, and is responsible for so much of why sales has a bad reputation. Everyone, at some point or other, has experienced or seen the stereotypical 'pushy salesperson' who doesn't care about your outcome, only their own:

- The door-to-door salesperson using slippery tactics to trick you into buying something that you otherwise wouldn't buy or don't need.
- The fit-pro trying to shame you into making your life better. This person isn't persuading you to buy from excitement, but fear. I don't know about you but I for one would *much* rather have people buy from me out of excitement, not because they are scared or worried about what will happen if they don't!
- The con-artist used car salesman. He doesn't care about the quality of your experience or what happens when you leave – he just wants your money.
- The gift of the gab Wolf of Wall Street type who will hoodwink you out of your hard-earned money by convincing you to buy something you don't want and didn't even know you needed.

**Truth:** Selling is how you let people know what is available and how to buy from you. If you want your business to have a good reputation and be filled with repeat clients you love to work with, I advocate for you selling by connecting on a human level, building relationships and offering information that aids decision making. Not a whiff of sleaze required. Promise!

## Myth 2: You need a big audience to make sales online

You know how it is – you're scrolling through Instagram and all you're seeing are business owners killing it on social media. You tell yourself they probably have more time than you, and they certainly have a bigger audience than you – so of course they're selling more than you! You tell yourself the reason your product isn't selling is because your audience is too small, and if you could just grow it, the sales would come rolling in, right?

I hear this *all the time* and it's just not the case. Where did it come from? Business owners do not need to go viral or have a huge social media following to make sales. This notion is bizarre, misleading and damaging for the small business community. It can lead you to believe that instead of a sales strategy, all you need is to grow or establish a big audience to earn money, when in fact the opposite is true.

**Truth:** The size of your audience doesn't determine how many sales, and how much money, you make. If you're not already making sales from the audience you have, you don't need to grow, you need to figure out how to sell to your existing audience first.

There are lots of online business 'gurus' who want you to believe that online business is *very, very hard* so that you feel over-whelmed and throw lots and lots of your money at them to get help. To be clear, you don't need thousands (or even hundreds) of followers, email sign ups or leads to make a *lot* of money and have a wildly successful and happy time in business. In fact, if you ignore all the noise and concentrate on what matters most, it's pretty simple. Taking regular sales action to bring in clients is key – if you have no clients, you won't have a business for very long!

And yet I see so many business owners putting off working on their sales plan because they believe their audience is too small, they should 'wait', or there is this notion that something else is more important than getting the right clients. This is self-sabotage at its finest. If you're in business and you don't have a big sales team doing this for you, you are the salesperson. *You* have to sell – there's nobody else to do it for you. And if you're delaying taking sales action because you are focusing on audience growth first, well, we need to talk.

I've worked with countless business owners to ensure their time spent on social media generates business, and what you *really* need is a solid handle on the way you generate interest for your skills and services (leads) and how you convert that interest into money in your bank (convert to sales). The combination of a sales plan and a social media presence will serve you well when used strategically together, and by the end of Part III, you'll know exactly how to do that.

Let me say it one more time before we move on – you don't need a bigger audience to make more sales for your business, you can (and should) start honing your sales skills right now. If you're not already getting sales, it's because you're not capturing the attention of the people who might want to buy from you. And that won't change no matter how large your audience is. Sell from day one.

I have worked with clients who have *huge* social media followings and aren't turning a profit, and equally with clients with *no* social media presence who are making hundreds and hundreds of thousands of pounds every year.

## Myth 3: Sales is purely transactional

This style of selling is based primarily on a business model that relies on the impersonal: churn and a steady stream of new one-off buyers – selling to someone once and then moving on. No need for personal touches or a lovely experience because you are never going to see them again.

If you are a small business owner, impersonal, transaction-based selling activities that don't consider the value of repeat clients, relationships or personal touches are not particularly useful. Stereotypes that spring to mind include the cold caller or someone sliding into your direct messages (DMs), who doesn't make the effort to know your name or anything about you, but asks you to buy from them anyway. This is not representative of heart-led, purpose-driven small business owners because it completely fails to take account of what most small business owners set out to do, which is to share experiences and to help people.

If you have set up a business doing the thing you love – be that creating your art and selling it, creating services to help other people, or putting together educational resources on specific topics, what you are selling *is* personal. You are not selling widgets to a faceless stranger via a third-party platform. You are selling *you*, and that makes this a completely different ballgame. We'll get into selling as a personal brand in Part III, but for now, just know that cold spammy selling is a completely different beast to what we're doing here.

**Truth:** Small businesses do not operate in the same way as large institutions, so neither should their sales strategies. Transactional selling wasn't made for businesses like yours and mine. And that's why it feels so jarring to the small business community, who operate on a much more personal, human-to-human level.

It is neither aspirational nor serving you to allow a version of selling that was born in big business boardrooms and pre-dates the internet, to be the dominant version in promoting your brilliant business in the online space. This is all the more true if you don't even *like* being sold to in that way! Taking on such an ill-fitting strategy would be as ridiculous as someone telling you had to wear 6-inch stilettoes to be successful, even if you hated wearing high heels. Trying to squidge your foot into 6-inch high heels and staggering around all day in them just because that's what you've seen other people doing would be madness, right? Surely we can all agree that that shoe just wasn't made for your trainer-loving tootsies, so free yourself from the drama of it all.

In the service arena, sales are made by building relation-ships in a structured way. Investing your time in connecting to and nurturing the people you want to work with instead of focusing only on why they haven't bought from you yet, will not only see your sales results improve, but also skyrocket your referrals, repeat business and reputation.

## Myth 4: Shouty extroverts make the best salespeople

I am often told by small business owners that they don't think they are the right personality type for selling, and I reckon it stems from another utterly ill-fitting concept, which is that selling is in some way about being gregarious or dominating conversations. This fake news causes people to hold back from actively participating in the promotion of their work, because they don't feel like it's for them. Since sales are essential for your business to survive, this is also sabotage running riot – again. We are all salespeople and we get to choose our own style of doing it. Embracing our authentic personalities is how we do that.

Truth: The best salespeople are the ones who are actually doing it, focusing on understanding the needs of their clients and responding from there. Listening is far more important than talking, because until you have got to know how you can help them, you can't offer any useful guidance on what might be right for them.

## Myth 5: Good products sell themselves

This one lives rent free inside lots of business owners' heads – the idea that if you have created something and it isn't flying off the shelves, it must be the product that's at fault.

I know for lots of creatives who don't feel like 'sales-people' it can be tempting to believe this. If you have ever wondered, 'Is it absolutely necessary for me to actively "sell" aka talk about my products a fair bit?', let me be clear: the answer is yes.

**Truth:** Sales don't happen automatically even if what you're selling is the best in the world. Sorry to break it to you but that's just not how online business works. No matter how good your product is, you have to actively get in front of the people it is right for and actively sell it. Nobody buys something they can't see. And furthermore, people buy from small businesses because they want an experience, not just a transaction. What separates the two is *you*. Turning up, talking about your products, spelling it out, serving your audience, helping them get to know you, *you*.

## Create your own sales truth

It's time to stop telling yourself selling is something that *other people do* and accept that selling is something *every* business owner must do. The more buyers can have the client experience of dreams, the faster we can make the sleazy seller trope a thing of the past.

Ready to be the alternative to the version of selling you have experienced first-hand and are totally tired of? Let's pave a pathway to success that *doesn't* rely on fear or shame tactics to force the sale, so you can make sure your clients feel looked after, even before they buy from you.

The vast majority of small business owners have personal drivers that are way more meaningful to them than purely making money. The idea of pushing people to buy something they don't want is the opposite of what the creative economy is all about. Say no to selling in this unnatural, unsuitable, outdated way – nobody wants to be 'sold to' like that anyway.

For the avoidance of any doubt:

| ✗ | ✓ |
|---|---|
| Your client doesn't want to be sold to via a script | They *do* want genuine interaction |
| Your client doesn't want to be another number | They *do* want to feel real human connection |
| Your client doesn't want a sale that is purely transactional | They *do* want an experience and the opportunity to have a relationship with your brand beyond buying from you once |

Shouty sales tactics might work for some, but they aren't going to fly for me, and likely, not for you either. You are not bound by boardrooms and hierarchies and instructions coming down the chain, so you get to decide on a higher standard of care for your clients. You get to leave all the sleazy stuff and instead create experiences that are an absolute *dream* for your clients, and that is your superpower.

As small business owners we don't have to push or persuade people to buy from us (thank goodness!). We have something much more compelling: passion and purpose and missions that are often much bigger than us. We have stories to share that connect us to others. We can build relationships and offer solutions.

Sell to the audience you have. Get clear about how to promote your products without the pressure of a large audience. Then, when that's working effectively, you can focus on growing your community from there.

**Helen Perry on ... selling to the audience you have.**
Helen is a marketing expert who shares her know-how to help small business owners create brilliant email newsletters, navigate social media, and more.

'Like many people – especially women – I'd long told myself a story that I was "bad at selling", that I "couldn't do it" and didn't feel comfortable trying. That selling is gross and uncomfortable. Let me save you some time and tell you that all of those things are wrong. They were wrong for me and they're wrong for you. *Anyone can sell.*

When I started my own creative marketing business I realized I was going to have to get over myself and learn! If other people can sell their product, then so can I or you. Understanding the blocks we have around selling helps to dismantle them.

Selling is a discipline that can be learned like any other. It's a matter of first deciding to believe that what you are selling is valuable, helpful and worth the money (it is!). Then understanding who it can help, what results and feelings they are seeking and how your product provides the answer. You have to stretch your comfort zone. And you get better at it every time (and the only way to improve is to keep doing it).

What I sell is not the same every month. I work around school holidays and so does most of my customer base. So I plan to sell 3–4 "big" courses per year plus around a dozen smaller masterclasses. So weeks can go by when I'm not really "selling" anything. That's when I share marketing content like email newsletters and podcasts that keep my audience "warm" so they'll be more inclined to buy when I do have a launch. I've found the key to success with this kind of sales strategy is to keep talking about it and hold your nerve.'

 **Helen's top tips**

A great small repeatable action is to keep inviting people onto your email marketing list. It's the absolute *best* place to sell from a content marketing perspective. People find me via Instagram, my podcast and personal recommendation, make their way on to my email list – then buy.

To anyone struggling to get started I would say this: the ick is a lie. There is nothing gross about telling people about your product so that they can decide whether or not it's right for them. The more comfortable you can be talking about your product, the more sales you'll bring in.

A useful phrase I share with reluctant sellers is 'selling is just telling': you are just showing up to tell someone about your great product – if you don't tell them, how will they ever know? You have to talk about your thing a lot a lot a lot before people hear the message and buy. Hold. Your. Nerve.

Helen is the host of the excellent 'Just Bl\*\*dy Post It' podcast. You can find her on Instagram @_helen_perry_ or at her website www.helen-perry.co.uk.

# Now it's your turn!

## To ditch the myths and sell to the audience you have

Out with the old: Which old myths about selling are holding you back? List out all the ways they are stopping you from taking action.

In with the new: It's time to replace those fusty old ideas and bring in some new beliefs about what it means to sell. To help with this, complete the following sentence:

*'I am committed to selling with integrity and doing it regularly because it will grow my business and that means I can... .'*

What 'new belief' do you choose to actively hold instead of the old ones you inherited? This could be an affirmation, a statement of fact or an intention – whatever suits you best.

Here are a few beliefs that help my clients, to get you started.

1. My business relies on the strength of my sales skills.
2. The more times I sell the more money I make.
3. I love to sell and my clients love to buy.
4. The easier I make it for clients before the sale, the easier it'll be for me after the sale.
5. It is my job to show up and sell every day so that my clients can find me easily when they are ready to buy.
6. The point of selling is to position my services, not to push people to buy them.
7. The better I get at selling the quicker my clients can make informed decisions that are right for them.
8. My clients deserve to have the best experience I can provide, not just after they've bought from me, but from the very first interaction with my business.

## Chapter recap

- Six out of ten small business owners aren't promoting their products on social media. If more of them had the confidence to do so, the effect on the economy would be huge.
- Sales stereotypes came almost entirely from big business boardrooms and bear no relevance to your lovely small business.

- You get to choose the way you sell – so choose a better standard for your clients than icky!
- How well your product is selling is a barometer of how well you're selling it. No matter how fantastic your product is, it won't walk itself onto the internet and into the arms of its dream buyer, so if you're using that fake notion as a yardstick – stop!
- Build your sales habit before growing your audience. Learn to sell to ten people before trying to sell to 1,000.

Now that you're liberated from the stereotypes that aren't serving you, let's make sure that you're taking action that's right for your stage of business. On to Chapter 3 to remove the guesswork and move forward with intention.

# Chapter 3
# Diagnose your sales problem

*Knowing how to share my passion in a way that my clients can relate to has completely changed the game.*
(Louisa Clarke, difficult conversations expert)

In my first year of business, I made a loss – 365 days of toil to end up with negative income. Now, part of that was because I spent so much on training and equipment (tens of thousands of pounds), but still. All that work. All that effort! All that time juggling my baby and retraining and finding my way with a new career. It didn't feel good, especially when the naysayers around me started asking if I was missing having a cushy banker's salary. Fast forward to a few years later, and the first time I tried to sell an online product. It completely flopped. Nobody bought it. Not one person. *Ouch!*

If there is anything more disheartening than pouring your heart and soul into something only to finally release it to the world and for the only thing to happen is… *nothing…* then please, let me know what it is.

When it's taking longer than you want to build traction, or for those times when comparisonitis has got the better of you, I want you to remember this: *We have all been there. In fact, it's normal!*

Yes it feels demoralizing at the time, but looking back I can see exactly why it happened: my messaging was duff. Duffer than duff, if we're being technical. Back then I was a wedding photographer and marketed myself as a 'natural wedding photographer'. I was trying to please anyone and everyone with that wishy washy description (what does natural wedding photographer even *mean*?) and it made my messaging vague and uncompelling. In Chapter 6 you'll discover how never to make that mistake, but for now let's not dwell on that.

Taking that messy action taught me, step by step, what works just as much as what doesn't. I was fully booked in no time, and in Part II I'll spell out how you can do the same.

Moral of the story: the best way to learn things is to actually *do* them. And if it doesn't go right the first time, do them again. It's what you do after the flop that matters. There is absolutely zero shame in launching something and not getting sales straight away. It's happened to every business owner I know! Nobody gets everything perfect on the first go, and having your own business is a crash course in learning that lesson.

Knowing what to do to get your brilliant creations sold, and you paid, can feel tricky – especially if you haven't done it before. If you don't yet feel natural selling, you aren't sure if you're doing the 'right' things or you just want to feel more confident that your sales process is robust in the experience it delivers, buckle up. In this chapter you will discover and understand the best next steps from where you are, *without* being overwhelmed.

*No more guesswork.*

If you are experiencing slow growth, sales seem to come in at random or you would like clients to find you more easily: you have a sales problem. And knowing what type of sales problem will give you the clarity you need to inform the action that will resolve that problem.

So, let's get to the bottom of why your services aren't selling as well as you would like, so that you can move forward with a plan. Because only by isolating the problem can we build a pathway to solve it.

## Discover your sales problem

If sales aren't coming in at the rate you'd like yet, if it feels like something that's hard to do or if it's taking too long to see results, there are a few areas we can start looking at for clues.

It may be that you aren't promoting what you do clearly enough, that your messaging isn't doing its job of positioning your offer with your audience as the solutions they're looking for, as was the case for me in my 'natural wedding photographer' days.

Or maybe you're selling in a way that doesn't suit you, and therefore it feels gross to you, which is putting you off doing it. Lots of clients come to me because although they have tried various sales activities, they have found what they're doing doesn't *feel* good. This makes it hard to show up and do it very often.

Perhaps your sales activity is happening at random rather than as part of a well thought-out sales process, and this is hindering the momentum you build with your audience.

Or maybe you're jumping in with the 'ask' before furnishing your audience with the information they'll need to make a decision (aka warming up your audience) first.

Let me talk you through each problem and how to solve it below.

## Sales problem 1: Over-delivering

Over-deliverers are most comfortable when they are helping others, and they spend more time giving free advice than promoting or being paid for their products and services.

### Is this you?

You enjoy supporting people however you can. Your focus up to now has been providing solutions to problems through your free content in the hope that it will make people who see it want to buy from you.

You give a lot, and your main focus so far when creating content is delivering value for your community. You have created multiple resources to help your ideal client, and regularly get messages from members of your community, asking for free advice which you're happy to give.

You have a tendency to over-deliver and under-sell. When it comes to talking about your products and services directly, you notice yourself holding back.

## The problem with this approach

At the present time your primary focus is on creating as much content as you can that delivers useful tips and free value. It's likely that this approach isn't making the impact you desire or translating to regular enquiries... yet.

You are starting to realize that no matter how much value you pack your content with, your audience doesn't automatically turn into paying clients as a result. Something is missing – but what?

There is too much free education and not enough decision support. The weighting of your current content is too heavily focused towards free tips and value and not centred enough around the customer journey as a whole: providing a service that warms up your audience and leads people to an easy yes or no about whether to buy from you. It isn't easy to progress beyond the free content and closer to your paid offers because you are not creating the space or the content for followers to do so.

You and your community are stuck creating/consuming a never-ending cycle of educational content, which isn't progressing to sales because what your audience needs is support that will help them make a decision.

The content that you created to help your audience, is actually overwhelming them with too much information. Their diligence to implement the tips you provide is met with your appetite to create more and so the cycle repeats. This is time consuming for you, and runs the risk of overloading them with things to implement without support.

Your audience comes online for connection and when they get it, they crave clarity about how your products may help them. Your ideal client is often time poor, overwhelmed and on social media with an attention span that is ever-decreasing. They want you to spell it out.

So, instead of giving away so much free value, create more content that intentionally spells out who your products are for, what they do and how they work. This is worth so much more to your audience as it can feel really overwhelming to know when is the right time to buy your products, especially if they haven't worked with an expert like you before.

By shifting your focus to sharing more information about what's possible for someone when they work with you, the transformation you provide inside your paid programmes, and how they will feel, you will demystify when is the right time to buy, empower more people to make an easy yes/no decision and your sales will naturally increase.

## Sales problem 2: Not selling enough, aka being a sales-phobe

Sales-phobes are held back by an abject fear of showing up that stops them from talking easily to their audience about the services they have created. This makes them less visible than required, slows down progress and causes the path to getting a sale to be very long.

### Is this you?

You don't identify as a salesperson because when you think of salespeople you immediately think of 'sleazy' people. The idea of being perceived as pushy or full-on by promoting your services and products terrifies you and has left you paralysed by a fear of being judged in the same way.

As a result, you tend to opt out of proactively selling your products and services. Up to now you have instead focused your efforts on making your products and services the highest quality offering they can be.

## The problem with this approach

You're waiting for people to find you on their own. You're feeling stuck, invisible and like nothing is happening as quickly as you would like.

You are heart-led, full of integrity and have a tendency to overthink when something feels scary or new. You have big goals for your business (and the notebooks full of detail to prove it!) but when it comes to promoting your ideas you have found yourself held back by fear. Fear of rejection, fear of what people will think, fear of not knowing what to do next, and that's just for starters!

You wish it could be easier finding clients because you love serving your people and the work that you do. Your work energizes you and you're hungry for more – you get genuine satisfaction and brilliant feedback, you're just not confident on the self-promotion front.

*Your products cannot sell themselves (no matter how great they are).*

*You* are what sells your products and services – especially in the first few years until momentum and word of mouth takes over.

*You* are what your audience wants to connect to first: your stories, visibility and the content you put out are what builds curiosity for your products and services.

*You* are the reason your followers will decide whether to progress to paying clients.

*If you don't show up, who will?*

Without you actively positioning your services, your audience can't receive the standard of care required to aid their decision-making process.

Your lack of visibility to connect with leaves your ideal client to navigate alone whether and when your services are right for them. This is an overwhelming task that carries several risks: making an inferior choice, having a disappointing experience or choosing to work with someone else purely because they had a more devoted approach to explaining their services through the content they put out on social media.

By not showing up to be the spokesperson for your products you put your integrity at risk – after all, your followers can't gain access to something if they don't know it exists, don't fully understand it or aren't confident in its ability to help them. So, can you afford *not* to ensure your social media content is delivering the key information about your paid products?

Being visible to guide people through your process will give more clarity, provide more connection to you and demonstrate confidence in your ability to help them.

- Selling with integrity means creating an experience that helps a potential client make an empowered decision that's right for them.
- Improving the way you feel about promoting your services even by a tiny amount will make a huge difference, so start small and build from there. Rather than thinking, 'Right, I need to do some selling today', try to think of this instead as 'How can I show up for my audience today in a way that feels aligned?'
- Commit to taking regular action to establish a routine for your sales activity. Focus on showing your passion for what you do.

## Sales problem 3: Sales enthusiast

Sales enthusiasts feel at ease selling and have had some 'OK' success in the past. The problem is: results are mixed. While they are strong at remembering to share links to buy things, the area they are lacking in is building genuine connection, which hinders results.

### Is this you?

You are excited about growing your business, and you talk about how people can work with you often. You keep your products and services visible and refer to them regularly. You know the success of your business hinges on how frequently you are able to generate leads, so you make sure your products are front of mind.

You may even have had formal sales training in the past, either pre-setting up your current business or in recent years via online 'guru' marketers. You might well have adopted strategies you've learned through courses, and despite following these to the letter, have not seen the instant flurry of new business you were expecting.

You don't always know how much personal content to include, so you tend to keep your content strictly focused on your products.

## The problem with this approach

It's too transactional. You spend a significant amount of time on sales calls with people who don't then go on to book you, which can leave you feeling disappointed that more of your conversations don't convert.

Your current focus leaves your content feeling quite 'samey' and repetitive. There is too much focus on 'getting the sale' and personal connection is lacking.

It is highly likely your tendency to only talk about your products is failing to pique your audience's interest – they need to establish connection with you before they're interested in what you're selling.

This is a problem for your business because connection, curiosity and demand are essential ingredients in making your 'pitch' highly desirable to the people who follow you. If you don't warm up your audience to you before inviting them to invest in your products and services, they cannot get to a place where they are ready to buy from you as quickly. No matter how many times you ask, your followers won't buy from you until they want to.

Focus on creating more content that explains who your products are right for, what result they can expect and how working with you works (more on this in Chapters 7–10). This creates more connection to your products, to you and to your ideal client's ability to make a change, and when you set up your content in this way, people can arrive at a place where they are ready to buy in a fraction of the time.

# Sales problem 4: Selling at random, aka flip-flopping

Flip-floppers haven't yet established a consistent pattern of sales activity and, as a result, there are often big gaps in between sales.

## Is this you?

You have found your ease with showing up and being visible online and enjoy social media for connecting with lots of different types of people.

You tend to adopt an 'all or nothing' approach to promoting – it's not that you mind promoting your products, it's more that you don't follow a clearly mapped out plan. As a result, progress happens in fits and starts, fluctuating with your energy.

You have lots of ideas and are prone to getting distracted. Your ambition means you compare yourself to your peers from time to time, which can lead to you wondering whether you 'should' be doing things in the exact same way as them. This can leave you overwhelmed, as you try things at random instead of keeping focused on creating or building your own recipe for success.

You know how important it is to be visible, but you sometimes feel like you are being vague or waffly. This causes you to overthink and has been known to spiral into a crisis of confidence where you feel unsure about why your content isn't connecting, unsure about what the best next step is, and lacking in clarity about your messaging.

It isn't unusual for you to wait for a return to feeling 'good' and for there to be long periods where you aren't promoting what you do, which affects the traction you're able to build.

The approach you have adopted up until now has led to some success, but you know it could be even better. If something is lacking, it's the consistency you crave in both sales and income.

## The problem with this approach

You are not talking about what's available often enough. This means that when you do take a sales action, it doesn't create a sale as readily. Because you are not promoting with regularity, your efforts can come out of the blue to your audience, which is jarring. Your lack of strategy and over reliance on natural inspiration is stopping you from creating consistent sales and messing with momentum.

Instead, commit to a set of repeatable actions you can take no matter what, and watch your traction grow. Warming up your audience happens by repeating the same key messages, month in month out, so your audience can feel clear about what you do and decide to buy from you when the time is right for them.

Say no to guesswork: know your sales problem and build your sales process from there. Clarity comes from action, but only if you're taking the right action for you!

### Louisa Clarke on ... removing guesswork by diagnosing her sales problem
**The power of positioning: from no prior sales experience to six figures in one year**

Louisa Clarke is a culture change consultant specializing in helping her clients handle difficult workplace conversations and advocate for themselves and their peers.

Louisa and I worked together to create a sales strategy that would increase her earnings as well as build her confidence with selling. At the start, Louisa told me she was overwhelmed with the noise online about what she 'should' be doing to make sales. Like so many others, she hadn't come from a background where sales and marketing were things she knew how to do, and after a few months of trying all of the things, Louisa knew it was time for a more productive approach. Putting out posts on social media and creating emails wasn't producing results because there wasn't a strategy in place to control what to post and when. As a busy mum to a preschooler and having quit her full-time job to go all-in on the business, the slow lane wasn't an option and, frankly, she didn't have the time or the inclination to mess around. She wanted to feel clearer about what was right for *her* business, how to articulate her passion in a way that would resonate with her clients, and to see faster traction and more sales.

We focused on:

- building simple, repeatable actions that built her sales confidence step by step;
- perfecting her positioning so that she was able to showcase who her services were right for more easily;
- creating more visibility in new places to start meaningful relationships with potential clients;
- using messaging and content proactively to help her audience understand how she could help them even with a product suite that had a wide range of potential applications.

I asked Louisa how she feels about selling now – this is what she said:

'This time last year I felt panicked. My business felt slow, I was trying things that weren't working and worrying that I wouldn't be able to make it work long term. The consistency, quality and ease of sales I have created now is light years apart. I'm in a great rhythm. I have a plan that drowns out the noise and keeps me feeling confident. I've doubled my target! At the start of this year, I set a sales target that felt lofty of £50k, and I've already made almost double that in the first five months. I've always believed in what I do, but knowing how to share my passion in a way that my clients can relate to so that they buy from me has completely changed the game.'

 **Louisa's top tip**

Get clear who you want to work with and commit to resonating with that group of people. Map out what you need to do in a way that's right for your business, because otherwise it's a lot of guesswork.

At the time of writing, Louisa posts on LinkedIn twice a week and has booked over £90k of work in the past five months, primarily through the precision of her positioning and clarity of her products. If that's not proof of the economic impact of sales confidence, I don't know what is!

Find Louisa on Instagram @confidentlythere and www.confidentlythere.com/ for a wealth of information about how to advocate for yourself, have difficult conversations and put in place strong boundaries.

## Now it's your turn!

### To say no to guesswork and diagnose your sales problem

Diagnose your sales problem by heading to my website and taking the free quiz, which you can find here: www.saradalrymple.

co.uk/moresalesplease along with all other resources that accompany this book.

*If you're over-giving*, focus on showcasing your ability to explain your products and who they are right for, so your audience are able to make easier decisions. Structuring your content in this way reduces the time it takes for a follower to progress to a stage where they are ready to buy from you. So, the easier you can make this process for them through your content, the more sales you will bring in. Looking back at the content you've created over the past month or so, have you spelled out what people can buy from you, how it works, and who your products are for? If not, home in on these points and make them the focus moving forward. Part II will help with this.

*If you're the sales-phobe*, focus on making yourself more visible to guide your audience through the decision-making journey. What small, new action can you introduce that will help your audience see you more easily? For example, you might start sending a more regular bite-sized snippet to your email list showcasing a certain product, you might create a frequently asked questions page for your website and direct people to it regularly, or perhaps you'll commit to sharing a tip on camera each week. Chapter 5 goes into more detail on the decision maker's journey.

*If you're the sales enthusiast*, focus on rebalancing your content so there's more focus on helping your audience understand how you can help them. Position what you do more precisely, so that it tells your audience what's in it for them. More on this in Chapter 6.

Invite your audience to ask you anything about your specialist topic and provide helpful responses, consider starting a weekly or monthly free Q+A that you host live, share the most common mistakes you see happening in your industry, or provide a useful time saver that your ideal client will benefit from. You are already a confident promoter, so adding in the simple step of hearing your clients tell you exactly what they want will vastly improve the relationships you make online, the quality of the conversations, and in turn the conversions you are having.

*If you're the flip-flopper*, focus on bringing more consistency into your action taking. It's much better to spend 10–15 minutes promoting simple, repeatable messages, every day for a month, than it is to push really hard just once or twice.

You will see more regular sales when you build regular sales action into your routine. Consistent sales takes are the result of consistent action, so to grow your business beyond where you are right now, your next step is to create more consistency and structure to your content. You'll discover how to make this as easy for you as possible in Parts II and III.

## Chapter recap

- Nobody gets things perfect on the first go, so if you've ever sold something to crickets: Welcome to the game! Don't give up, keep going until you crack it!
- The only way to learn how to do things is to actually do them (and to keep doing them).
- Remove the guesswork by understanding where you are in your sales journey right now, and build your plan of action from there.
- If every business owner was clear on the action to take and spent just a few minutes each day promoting their products, the impact on their bank accounts and the economy as a whole would be huge. Be more Louisa!

Now you know the main sales problems and how to overcome them, let's stack the deck in your favour by looking at how to maintain ease, whether your business is in its infancy or if you've been here a while. Because who wants business to be stressful? Not me.

# Chapter 4

# The non-negotiables of selling well

*The more you talk about what you do, the easier it gets.*
(Lou Chudley, Instagram trainer)

I burned out good and proper in 2021 and oof, I wouldn't wish it on anyone.

All of a sudden I went from being a mostly bubbly, energetic person to not enjoying very much at all. I couldn't enjoy anything the way I was used to, from my family to my work; it all just felt too exhausting. My sleep was disrupted, I had anxiety, my jaw got so sore from grinding my teeth every night that I would get headaches, I couldn't switch off. It was horrific to be honest!

It might sound silly to say this, but it was the first time in my 40 odd years I really clocked that my ability to earn money depended so wholly on me being OK. When you are employed, you have access to sick pay when you're unable to work, but when you are a business owner, that's not so straightforward. It was really scary to watch my earning potential fizzle out as my energy left the building. Yep, you could say I found out the hard way that treating your energy like your most precious asset is the single most important thing you can do for your business.

# My burnout story

As an extrovert I am most energized when I'm around people – talking to them, hearing a variety of stories, chewing the cud. Having the option to spend time with people as I normally would had a huge impact on me and my energy levels.

Burnout came knocking about a year into the coronavirus pandemic, in 2021, when my kids had been at home every day for nine months out of 12, when my husband and I had been tag teaming getting up at 5am/working late shifts to honour our work commitments, when there was no spare time for down time at all, and when the stress of home schooling had us all perplexed over frontal adverbials and goodness knows what else.

(If you also lived through the lockdown era with young children and enjoyed the very special extra gift of home schooling, you will know exactly what I mean when I say It… Was… Relentless.) But even if you didn't – it's still relevant, promise!

Home schooling two children of seven and four alongside work had used up every crevice of time available, and after nine months or so as a makeshift teacher, family cook and business owner, I was ready to slide down the wall and not get up again for a really long time.

For the first time ever, my energy flatlined. I'd gone from growing a thriving business of mentoring clients that I loved, to all of a sudden barely having minimal energy levels to sustain myself, my family or my business. Turns out there's only so much pushing through it you can do before you hit the pavement.

It took almost a whole year to get back to 'normal'. Almost a year of not being able to do the things I loved in the way I wanted to do them. Almost a year of my earnings being affected by my inability to 'show up' in the same way. Almost a year of worrying about what would happen. Almost a year of wondering what on earth was going on.

So, do you want to know my first rule for making lots of sales and sustaining your business long term?

*Do not – under any circumstances – leave yourself open to burnout.* Burnout is one of the biggest risks, both to your ability to make sales and your business' long-term success. I've written this chapter to help you get the benefit of my experience, and the foundations of making sales without burning yourself out.

## What burnout risk is and how to avoid it

Burnout is a syndrome caused by chronic work-related stress.[1] According to a 2019 study, 48% of small business owners had experienced burnout in the previous year.[2]

From income uncertainty to decision fatigue, alongside balancing domestic load, business owners are exposed to a variety of potential stressors and triggers. These are exacerbated by the fact that many business owners rely almost exclusively on their own experience, skills and motivation day to day.

Entrepreneurship brings new challenges that you may not have dealt with before – especially if your previous work experience was in a more corporate setting. One of the biggest is fluctuating income, especially in the beginning. Unstable income is one of the biggest stressors on business owners in the first few years.

I'm going to level with you: left to its own devices, your business won't hesitate to gobble up all your time, drag you around energetically and drain you dry of resources. And I'm not just talking about down the line, that can all happen even *before* you hit profitability.

---

[1]  www.who.int/news/item/28-05-2019-burn-out-an-occupational-phenomenon-international-classification-of-diseases

[2]  www.uschamber.com/co/grow/thrive/entrepreneur-burnout-stress#:~:text=However%2C%20burnout%20isn't%20felt,year%2C%20a%20recent%20survey%20found.

One minute you're starting a fun new venture, and all of a sudden, you're up to your eyes in to-do list, you're responsible for about eleventy billion extra decisions that need to be made every week, you don't have a team to soundboard against, you're worrying about how to replace your old income ... it never stops and it can feel like a *lot*.

This is even more true if you're adding your business to additional caring responsibilities, chronic illness or a vibrant life outside of your business, where you are required to show up for other people even when you are not working. Most people don't set up in business to have it be something they are always 'on' for, and yet that quickly becomes the default setting.

I always tell my clients that selling is an exchange of energy: you share your positive energy for the thing you do, and it is met by the people who respond to it. So, what do you do when your energy has run a mile in the opposite direction?

## An easier way to sell

In burnout you can't even think about showing up to promote your business. Even if you manage to drag yourself online, your efforts won't produce the results you hope for, because the energetic piece isn't there to bring life to what you're saying and connect with your audience. In my experience with it, all you want to do is lie down and sleep for a hundred years. Not an option for me with two young kids in lockdown, and probably not particularly practical for you either. Basically, burnout pinches your ability to make money right from under your nose.

As I came to terms with being the person who had the energetic capacity of a sloth, I realized something. I didn't want to do any more 'launching' in a way that involved lots of prep and ramping up. The available time I had was so much less than before, so I had to find a way to use it more potently. I simply didn't have the energy to continue running my business in the same way I had done before. Forcing myself through multiple calls a day because I didn't want to let anyone down was a one-time-only-situation-never-to-be-repeated.

It was the catalyst for change. I knew I wanted to have fewer constraints on my calendar. I cleared my diary. I switched up the way I worked with people so it was less call-intensive. And, I developed my own, much simpler way of promoting my business.

Contrary to everything I'd been 'taught' by the online business experts I'd been learning from, I found that the complex launch methods I'd been making my way through weren't the only way to plentiful sales. I could share with my audience the information that would help them make purchasing decisions, *in just a few minutes each day.*

Even better - I realized it was infinitely more *fun* to sell in this freeing way. No more endless to-do lists, email sequences or 'rules', just simple, repeatable actions that could deliver clear messaging over and over again. Marvellous stuff!

*If only I had realized this was an option sooner!*

Clients were in my messages responding more enthusiastically than ever. It was like a light switch had been turned on: I finally let it be easy! And the best part was, I could do it every day in a matter of minutes!

Mastering everyday selling in a way that felt genuinely fun and easy was key for me being able to sustain my energy and my business during that time, and I've never looked back.

Burnout took my capacity right down to a fraction of what it was before. It forced me to focus on what my absolute non-negotiable work tasks are and to ditch everything else. It reminded me how much of an energy game selling is and I have to be grateful for that.

| Goodbye | Hello |
|---|---|
| ✘ Complicated launch plans | ✔ Simple, repeatable actions |
| ✘ Filling the diary with calls | ✔ Filling the diary with space |
| ✘ Following other people's rules | ✔ Creating my own rules |
| ✘ Conversion focused | ✔ Experience focused |
| ✘ Depleting energy | ✔ Protecting energy |
| ✘ Posting random content in a non-strategic way | ✔ Creative content to aid the decision-making process |
| ✘ Scrolling social media for inspiration | ✔ Working on product clarity |
| ✘ Waiting and hoping for clients to find you | ✔ Getting visible in intentional way |
| ✘ Big launch energy | ✔ Everyday selling |

My business is now all the better for it. I am a different business owner now. I am wildly efficient. I don't waste the time I have because I don't want to squander what it affords me: lots of space and time off. And everything is lighter as a result – I have more free time now than ever before.

What I learned was, the more you focus on making promoting simple, natural and something that feels as automatic as brushing your teeth, the easier your business gets to be.

So, how can we protect your number one asset – your available energy and the time you have to spend working – from its arch nemesis – burnout – and ensure you maintain the energy required to go the distance? By bringing your needle movers into sharp focus, that's how!

## Everyday selling

Burnout or no burnout, if you're anything like me, you'll have days where you have hours to work on your business and days where you're running around doing all sorts of work and non-related things that leave you squeezed on time.

Time and available energy are always fluid, so something that helps me stay at ease is prioritizing the tasks that I know feed the business. I don't want to have a business that grinds to a halt because I spent too long sending emails or playing around with a sales page. I want to know that sales come in no matter what. This means knowing the activities to focus on and prioritizing these helps me stay efficient. No matter what, I start with the needle movers: knowing these are done in the first hour of my day means that no matter what happens after that, I'm good.

I know, I know, when you have your own business there's always something you 'could' be doing. But I can happily confirm that there are actually very few things that you 'need' to do when it comes to promoting your products. That said, there are some actions to do if consistent sales and a thriving business full of clients you love working with is your goal. These key activities need to be done regularly and consistently: taking random, occasional action won't cut it. There needs to be a process and an order to the way you approach this.

To lead your business and grow your sales without having to work more, do more or be more, then getting to a place where you can promote your products in minutes a day will help you immeasurably.

Everyday selling is knowing the difference between the activities that will help your audience decide whether to buy from you, and the many, many ones that won't. It is committing to keeping the experience for your audience and your buyers as straightforward, fun and easy as possible so that nobody has to guess at whether you can help them, how you can help them, or what investing with you will be like. It is the most efficient form of promoting your business because you can do it from wherever you are, even on busy days, without needing anyone else or any other systems. It is high converting: it works!

When you do this, you become very clear very quickly how to share your stories with confidence and in your natural style. You improve quickly and your audience is not confused about what is available. As a result, sales happen easily. When you do it regularly as a top priority, you no longer waste time doing the many things that don't aid a sale, won't make you money, and can't help your clients get the results they want.

## Know your needle movers

### The non-negotiables of selling well

Prioritizing these actions has absolutely transformed my business and now I'm passing them on to you. These are the needle-moving tasks that will grow your business and your economic power. They keep promotion consistent, efficient and effective, no matter how much 'life stuff' is going on behind the scenes.

### 1. Create an experience you love

Sales is an exchange of energy. If you love what you're selling, that's what you'll lead with and people will pick up on it. I'm not talking 'that'll do', I'm talking be *obsessed* with the services you send out the door. Because if you're not, how can you expect your audience to be? It's a lot easier to sell something you love than something you don't! In Chapter 1, Lara showed us how she created the sell-out networking event Hugs and Brunch from a place of love.

### 2. Sell to the audience you have

Never put off talking about what you do because you're on a quest for a bigger audience: selling starts on day one in your business. The better you can become at talking about your products to your first ten potential clients, the easier you'll find it to talk to bigger audiences down the line. It also doesn't matter how humungous your audience is if you don't actually know how to sell to them. So, wherever you're at in business right now, start selling today. In Chapter 2, we saw how selling should begin on day one of business, because until you can sell to ten people, you won't be able to sell to hundreds, or even thousands.

### 3. Remove the guesswork

Guesswork doesn't sell. It is also one of the biggest energy drains there is. Trying to fathom what's going to get you noticed by your ideal clients without support or a plan to get you there is a *lot* of work. It also takes a long time. So, no more winging it or trying any old thing in case it works! Diagnose your sales problem, set your next goal and create the corresponding plan of action from there. As Louisa shared in Chapter 3, diagnosing her sales problem and perfecting her positioning led to her hitting six figures in year one of business.

### 4. Know your needle movers

Save your energy: use your time wisely. As a business owner it's important to use your available energy for maximum benefit. Focus on the skills that matter, even the ones that feel 'hard' at first, and you'll quickly become quicker and find them easier. Use the ten non-negotiables of selling well as your guide (the list you're reading right now!).

### 5. Be easy to buy from

Be the solution to a specific problem and create a buying experience that is straightforward in helping the people you want to work with arrive at a decision to buy. This isn't only based on logic – you also need an emotional connection. In Chapter 5, branding coach Helen Bamborough talks about ways you can use your brand to create an experience your clients will love.

### 6. Be visible

This may sound obvious, but if the way that you are promoting your business is online, then make sure you are showing up and being seen there. Your clients want to buy from *you*, and in order to do that they need to see *you* so that they can build that all important know, like and trust factor that starts off the connection that turns into the relationship that ends with a sales decision being made. The more people can see and get to know you, the more sales you will make. And the good news is, the more you do it the easier it feels! Chapter 6 is packed with tips to help your visibility efforts.

### 7. Have a plan – and stick to it

Create a set of simple, repeatable actions that advocate for what your client wants. This will help your audience understand whether your products are for them. This is what creates efficiency and saves time. The magic of social media is in using it to deliver key messages in a routine way, and then getting on with your day. Without a plan you're open to changing direction, comparisonitis and feeling overwhelmed. In Chapter 7, you will hear from Lucie Sheridan how building her step-by-step sales plan allowed her to double her target.

### 8. Be yourself

Online marketing is 50% what you're selling, and 50% who you are as a business owner and human being. Clients buy into you first, then your products. Sharing pieces of information that help people get to know who you are helps your audience connect to you. And when we feel connected to you, we are already more interested in hearing more about what your business does. Harnessing the power of personal brand is where it's at if you want to stand out. In

Chapter 8, we will hear how Lucy Werner used hers and diversified her income.

### 9. Create content to match the stages of the sales process

There is a big difference between chucking something up on your social media feed because you know you 'should' and posting with a plan. One leads to endless hours wasted and no sales, and the other calls your people closer and helps them buy from you. Your content should never be filler. Chapter 9 is devoted to making this a doddle.

### 10. Sell every day

Present your offer and give regular opportunities for people to buy it, so that when the time is right for them, they can. Nobody buys the first time they see what's available! People need time to get to know your products, and talking about them often is how you help that happen. The compound effect of your daily sales activity is so much more powerful than any one piece of content can ever be. In Chapter 10, you will find the daily prompts that will help you take action in 30 minutes max each day.

Will these ten things bring you thousands of sales on day one? No. Will they help you make promoting your business something you can do effortlessly, in the natural rhythm of your working day, without batting an eyelid so you can increase your sales? Absolutely yes.

Know your needle movers – the non-negotiable activities to spend your time on, aka the key actions you take to bring sales into the business. Without these actions, there is no business!

### Lou Chudley on ... knowing her needle movers

Lou Chudley is an Instagram trainer who has built a thriving business, Spark Social, through regularly being visible on camera on social media and talking about how she can help small businesses.

'I realized soon after starting my Instagram training business, Spark Social, that being visible was going to be a key needle mover and knowing that it would help people decide whether I'm the right choice for them was a huge motivator. I know it helps me connect to more people, stand out and makes my business more memorable. Being able to "meet" me online first has a huge impact on my sales.

I had to practise being so visible and showing my face on social media because it didn't feel natural at first, but now it takes me a lot less time because through showing up so regularly over a period of time I've become much more succinct and clear in my messaging.

I don't think posting every day or the size of your audience is half as important as people think – I've found what matters most is the quality of connection you have with the people in that audience. Taking time to get to know people instead of treating them like just another number is something I love to do, and I know my clients love. I'd much rather post high-quality content that helps my audience than whizzing something out the door for the sake of it.

My non-negotiable daily activity is talking about what I do – this is the important thing because people don't know in real time how they can work with me if I don't keep the information front of mind for them. I know my audience are busy and I don't want to make it hard for them to remember when my workshops and trainings are taking place. I spend at least 50% of my time marketing and selling my services. The more time I spend doing this, the clearer my message gets and repeating it as much as possible is key.'

 **Lou's top tips:**

The things that have helped me the most are: practising! The more you talk about what you do, the easier it gets. I focus on getting to know my audience so that I can speak in a way that resonates with them and I make it really clear what problem I'm solving with each of my workshops. Don't assume everyone has seen you talk about your offer – they haven't.

If you're feeling shy – collaborate. Do a joint live on a certain topic, interview each other, or write up a piece together. Showing up with someone you already know as a joint visibility effort feels so much more natural and gets you both in front of each other's audience – win win!

Lou's account is @sparksocial on Instagram, or visit her website www.spark-social.co.uk/ for inspiration on how to get visible.

# Now it's your turn!

## To know your needle-movers and use your time wisely

Print off the 'Non-negotiables of selling well' poster (you can find it along with all other accompanying resources for the book here: www.saradalrymple.co.uk/moresalesplease) and stick it up somewhere you can see it, to remind you of your top ten tasks. Which of them do you already confident about, and which ones do you feel you need to get better at? Note down the ones you feel are a top priority, and as you go through the rest of this book, highlight the relevant areas to support you.

How can you allocate more time to the needle-moving activities of promoting, selling and marketing? Blocking out 30–60 minutes a day in your diary is a great way to boundary the time.

## Chapter recap

- Sales is an energy exchange, so if you have no energy, you have nothing to exchange! Therefore, having a streamlined set of actions will help you avoid burnout.
- Without keeping an eye out, your business will happily steal all your time and energy, so it's important to be intentional and keep space for key actions.
- There are ten non-negotiable activities when it comes to selling well: prioritize them.
- Ensure you have time blocked in your diary for promotional activity. As a guide, at least 50% of your available business time should be spent on sales and marketing.

And that's it! Part I is done. You've identified how common yet outdated myths about selling are holding you back, diagnosed your sales problem and got clear on the main activities that drive sales and are therefore now your main focus, your non-negotiables. I bet you're already feeling clearer about what to do and why!

Now let's build your confidence further by mapping out the steps to take, one by one. Your sales process gives you the confidence you need to get visible. It is the structure that protects you from burnout and ensures you create the sales you desire in the time you have available, so let's skip on into Part II and get into it! Bye-bye sales myths and pushy stereotypes, hello ease, consistency and client attraction!

# Part II

# More sales confidence

If you have ever felt as though you are 'winging it' when it comes to sales, or you don't feel completely confident that what you're doing is working, then this part is for you!

The next three chapters are a giant boost of confidence that walk you through how to get visible with ease. We're walking through the foundations of selling with integrity, the four stages of selling and creating your plan of action. When you have a plan, you feel more confident and when you feel more confident it's much easier to show up and be seen.

The next three chapters will ensure promoting and selling your products is something you feel totally confident you know how to do. From the foundations to the step-by-step strategy, to how to position your products with precision every time, you'll pave the way to enable clients to say yes with a new level of conviction. This is where we say goodbye to guesswork and build your roadmap, brick by brick, so that your sales process is complete, efficient and effective.

Read on if you're ready to learn how to:

1. make sustainable sales and earn consistent income so that your business survives (and thrives!) long term – yes please!
2. create your set of simple, repeatable actions that won't make you want to collapse in a burned-out heap;
3. design the entire process to feel natural and right for you;
4. ensure your audience can make easy decisions about whether to buy from you;
5. not feel like a total twit while you're doing it.

When you're done you'll have your sales actions set and ready to implement on social media in Part III.

# Chapter 5

# The decision maker's journey

*A good brand is instantly recognisable as your own, reflects our personality and talks to the people you want to call in.*
(Helen Bamborough, creator of bold brands)

In the early 2000s I spent my days watching *Popstars: The Rivals*, dancing in clubs that were inhumanely sweaty and, for a few hours a week, holed up in lecture theatres studying for an Economics degree at the University of Nottingham. My favourite modules were all the ones about people: from the labour market to the supermarket – I was fascinated. (Do you know how much thought goes into what products are put at eye level vs those above and below? It's a lot.)

In Behavioural Economics, we analysed the decisions made by consumers. At that time, it was widely supposed that human decision is highly rational, i.e. determined predominantly from a place of logic. Every step assumed, mapped out, put into a fancy graph or equation, right there on the blackboard. And from there the much cleverer-than-me economists could – and did – extrapolate out how they believed people in different demographics would behave. Whether that was in the labour force, in the home, what they would choose to buy at the shops, you name it, there was an assumption and an equation for it.

At around the same time as I was being somewhat bamboozled by unlikely economic theories about the ever so rational behaviour of human decision making, a business professor sat across the pond at Harvard School of Business writing a paper that would go on to disprove that theory completely. Gerald Zaltman found that when it comes to decision making it is not pure logic, but in fact our emotions, that play the predominant role in most of the decisions we make, every day.

Zaltman found that 95% of purchase decisions are made by the subconscious, in a part of the brain called the limbic system.[1] He proved that emotions drive purchasing behaviours. What these findings translate into for us as business owners is this: people are led by their emotions first when they buy, and then once the emotional connection has been made, logic then steps in to perform the role of sense checking everything. Not the other way round.

Basing a sales effort on logic alone is a sure-fire way to scupper your sales. When you do this, the vast majority of your audience will get bored long before getting anywhere close to wanting to buy from you. If our sales activity is made up solely of talking about features, attributes and other logic-based information about our products and services, it will fail to supply the emotional links required to connect with the consumer. The emotional connection that exists between you and your client must be established before the features or details of your specific services will capture attention. It is the emotion or sense of feeling that fuels a purchasing decision.

This point explains why things don't always sell out the minute you launch them, why your audience won't buy something you're not setting into context, and why simply talking about the practical features of your product or service isn't enough.

Selling was never supposed to be a 'one and done' situation, so if you've ever mentioned your product once online and felt deflated if it didn't sell straight away, take solace in the fact that's just not how it works. That would leave no role for personality in the process. Which would not only be dull as dishwater, but also it makes it really hard to distinguish one option from another and connect with what you're buying.

---

[1] Gerald Zaltman, How Customers Think: Essential Insights into the Mind of the Market (Harvard Business School Press, 2003).

The rest of this book will show you how to use social media as a way to create emotional connection first, then to back it up with information that is logical and required to arrive at decision making so that the journey you take your buyer on is useful, personality fuelled and enjoyable for all parties.

## Who is a buyer? Who is not a buyer?

When a buyer has considered their options, they will make a decision that either ends in a 'yes', a 'no' or a 'not right now'.

Remember: you are not trying to win over everybody on the internet and have every single person who comes across your page buy from you. That would be unrealistic and exhausting. You are only looking to call in the people who are right for your products, right now.

Your buyer **is not**:

- someone who is in the type of situation you know you can help with but who is not yet financially ready to buy;
- someone who is in the type of situation you know you can help with but who is not interested in fixing their problem;
- someone who is in the type of situation you know you can help with and who has the financial means to pay you but who is not yet ready to buy.

Your buyer **is**:

- *actively looking* for the very thing you sell;
- ready to move right now;
- someone who has both the motivation to make a change and the means to make that change happen.

Selling is not about convincing someone to buy something they don't want – we are only looking for the people who *do* want what you have to offer. The goal with your sales process is to provide a pathway that facilitates easy decision making for all, and to combine it with a service so thorough that each individual can make up their own mind with conviction.

## The decision maker's journey

As you will already, I'm sure, have realized, there's more to making sales than simply setting up a website, plonking your stuff onto it and waiting for people to find it and buy.

In Chapter 1, we defined the sales process as the set of actions you take to make a buying decision easy for clients. The goal is to empower your audience to make the right choice for them and to feel really good about making that choice. To do this you must walk people from a place of not knowing you or your business at all to being ready to decide whether (or not) to buy from you.

The decision maker's journey is the journey a potential client takes between finding you and making a decision about whether to buy from you. It can be summarized simply as 'the customer's path to purchase'. During this process they research a problem, find potential solutions to it, and then choose one of those solutions.

First, people need to know you exist. Then, when they've found you, they need to build an emotional connection to you and your products. This happens through the information you share online. Your content does the job of nurturing or 'warming up' your client and without it, the sale would be happening cold: it would be purely transaction based, logic focused and highly impersonal. Since that is not the style of selling most of us enjoy to put out or to receive, we instead focus on facilitating the decision-making process, aka the buyer journey. Then, when they feel connected to you on a human level, their interest in how they can buy from you increases.

The activity we take in our sales process should meet our clients exactly where they are, all the way from their very first introduction to the work we do, right through the journey they take to making a decision to buy or not. Our unique opportunity as small business owners is to make the buyer's journey as easy as possible using human connection, stories and just being ourselves. The goal is not to achieve a sale every time, but to empower clients to make enthusiastic, full-bodied decisions without force or push.

**THE DECISION MAKER'S JOURNEY**

**1 INITIAL DISCOVERY**
Person finds you for the first time, through your visibility efforts online or in real life.

**2 RELEVANCE**
The first thing a new person into your world wants to know is: what's in it for them?

**3 AUDIENCE NURTURING**
Once relevance is established, client next looks to see whether they connect with you on a more personal level. They do this through your content.

**4 CONVERSATIONS**
If the person consuming your content is looking for what you're selling, understands your product and connects with you personally, they will look to speak to you directly.

**5 EXPERIENCE**
Through the conversation that ensues, they determine what kind of experience you will provide and make a decision from there.

Creating an easy process for your customers to follow will not only improve their experience, it will also make you more sales.

The key phases of the journey to a decision are shown in the diagram. When you set up your buyer experience in line with these steps, you ensure you are creating a point of connection between you and your audience. From there you can back up with logic and your client can progress to a decision they feel confident about.

## What drives a sale?

Zaltman showed us that emotions drive purchases, but what does that actually *mean*? It means our urge to buy something usually comes from a desire to make improvements, that's what. We as humans have a right royal penchant for wanting things to be better than they are right now.

Ninety-five per cent of buying decisions are driven by the emotional areas of our brain (the limbic system).[2] In almost no cases is a purchase driven by low-vibe emotions or solely logic. We all have things we want to be better at, have more of, do more efficiently or by using less personal resource. Our role as business owners is to understand what drives the purchase of our own services.

Seventy-one per cent of people base their buying decisions on trust and believability, and there are two main frequencies that trigger a purchase:

- to solve problems (70%);
- to gain something they desire to have (30%).[3]

---

[2] Gerald Zaltman, How Customers Think: Essential Insights into the Mind of the Market (Harvard Business School Press, 2003).
[3] www.impactcommunicationsinc.com/pdf/nwsltr_2001/ICINwsltrpr 0108.pdf

When we know how our products fit with what our clients want, we can create a sales process that actually serves to aid decision making rather than one that's based on luck, wishful thinking or pushy tactics. Is your product there to solve a problem, is it to help your client achieve a perceived status or feel a certain type of way?

By the time the conscious mind is making a choice, you will typically already feel a pull or have a gut feeling about whether to buy. This is because the decision has usually already subconsciously been made based on emotion. This explains, for example, why consumers so often choose more expensive products even when there is a cheaper, more generic version available. Think about how many people are walking around with iPhones, Airpods and Macbooks. People love buying from Apple and certainly not because it's the cheapest option around.

Similarly in the high-end fashion space, you might look at the price of a designer handbag, versus a label-free version that can be bought for a fraction of the price. The price is not the determining factor in the high-end purchase, it is the label, brand loyalty, perceived quality and status that draws people in. The same is also true in your business, but only if you give people a brand experience to actually enjoy and become loyal to!

Humans connect emotionally: we are attracted to other humans or brands who have the same set of values as we do. This provides small business owners the very real benefit of creating a decision-making process around human connection.

We can comfortably say that in the small business space in particular, the relationship between the consumer and a small business is formed out of a collection of mutual experiences, connection points and feelings. Therefore, there is no need to make selling anything other than sharing information that's genuine, inviting connection to be unearthed where it already exists, and leading with personality over pressure.

- Share your values: Buyers like to buy from sellers they can connect with over mutual values or ideals. Whether through your personal brand, your brand story, or your visual brand, sharing the values you run your business by and the reason your business exists will help people connect on a much more genuine human level.

- Keep your customer at the heart of all you do: Truly understand who your customer is and why they want to interact with you. Understanding their drivers and behaviours on an emotional level will help you adapt all your touchpoints to target them specifically.
- Branding and design: The visual aspects of the online experience you create add an overall 'vibe' which consumers are influenced by on an emotional level. Consider the impact your branding has in evoking positive emotions, mutual commonality and personal context. From colour to structure, imagery, fonts and personalization, all touchpoints of your brand when used in a cohesive way can create emotional engagement.

## Be easy to buy from

Having an online presence centred around human connection is a huge driver of sales. Research suggests that 81% of shoppers look online before deciding to buy and 74% rely on social media to guide purchasing decisions. That's almost three-quarters of buyers that expect you to be there![4]

Your products and services will often be created without any personal input from each specific client, which makes it very important that you explain to your audience exactly what each offering exists to do, and who for. This is a large part of the process and a really key reason to show up consistently.

Because your range of options is (largely) created in advance, your role is to support your potential buyer at every stage, to help them understand what each option is and how it may/may not be suitable for them in respect of their unique needs. Your service is to understand the requirements, provide clarity and

---

[4] www.businessdit.com/small-business-online-marketing-statistics/

your expert opinion on a range of suitable options, and to let them choose from there.

It's important to showcase yourself as the expert in your own services and to lead your clients to understand whether they'll get what they want and need from your service. It's your responsibility to make recommendations that are suitable for them, not theirs to figure it all out for themselves.

Therefore, it's in everyone's best interests that you show up consistently in pursuit of providing absolute clarity to your audience, even in the beginning when it doesn't feel natural to do so. Your clients are always online – we are not in control of when they are browsing their options or when they are not. It's not like having a physical shop that you can open and close. The information they find when they arrive at your social media page or website needs to meet people at all stages of the journey, and your content plays a large role in meeting people wherever they are. You'll discover more about how to do this in Chapter 7.

# Establishing suitability: why getting a no is no bad thing!

There's a lot of focus on getting the 'yes' when it comes to the literature around selling. I invite you to welcome getting a 'no' just as much. Far from being something to fear, a 'no' is a crisis avoided and seeking it out will save you from growing a business that makes you miserable.

To make my point, let's explore a hypothetical scenario. Let's imagine for a moment that every single person who found you online automatically wanted to buy from you, just like that. Sounds great, right? Actually, wrong.

It is in your best interest to use your sales process to assess suitability and arrive at a no if it's not.

A no is not about you, it's about ensuring suitability and best outcome for the client. The better you are at doing this, the higher the percentage of happy clients you will have and the better your business will be.

Your experience matters just as much as your clients. And it's not just a nice to have, there is huge value in it, too. Your energy needs to remain high in order for you to continue producing.

If you are a service provider, and you work with clients over a longstanding period of time, the suitability of your clients for the services you're selling them has a binary impact on what they get out of their time with you (and you them). You have very limited time and energy and you want to save it for amazing clients *only*. So, filling your business with any old Tom, Dick or Harry that comes along carries nasty risks to your reputation, to your experience, and to the way your business progresses.

Saying yes to everybody leaves you open to working with a good number of people who just don't value what you do. If suitability is not established in your sales process, you'll be in a contract you can't fulfil with a client who will never be happy with you. This leads to dissatisfied clients, additional stress and refund requests. It also feels ghastly to fill your business with clients who don't value what you do.

*So, if they are not the right fit for right now for your product, if you are not the right expert for them, if you cannot get them closer to the result that they want or need, a no is a good thing. If they are not your dream client, if something doesn't feel right, if there is a red flag, a no is a good thing. Protect your energy, always.*

Now let's consider the alternative, which is that your sales process makes it straightforward and instantly clear to your audience exactly who you are calling in for each product or service, and who you might not be such a good fit for.

In this case, the people who decide to book calls with you, messages you or get in touch to pay you outright, have already self-selected because they are clear and informed. Instead of spending half your life on calls helping people decide what's right for them or not (and feeling icky in the process) you have helped all parties in an efficient way. The clients you *do* work with are delighted by the experience they get, because they are the perfect match for you and appreciate the extra touches and additional things over and above your expertise that you bring.

 Be easy to buy from. Use your brand to foster emotional connection at each stage of the decision maker's journey.

## Helen Bamborough on ... leveraging your brand, creating an emotional connection and being easy to buy from

Helen Bamborough is a brand and positioning coach who helps her clients reveal strong identities to create elevated client experiences based on genuine connection. I asked her to shed some light on how to use branding to improve connection – and here's what she said:

'Good branding weaves your personality, identity and experience through all stages of the decision-making process. It helps you stand out, grab the attention of ideal clients and make a lasting impression on your target audience. Creating a well thought-out brand has helped me stand out as a premium service provider and to price accordingly, and it will absolutely do the same for you!

Confused branding on the other hand, will do your clients and your products a disservice by diluting the power of your message. One of my biggest bugbears is lack of clarity and I hate seeing people buy things they don't need or aren't ready for out of confusion or bad advice. I create experiences that help my clients make decisions that are right for them and to feel really good about that. I absolutely love personalized, five-star experiences so I use branding to do that for my clients, too. I know that the easier I can make it for people to know how I can help them, and how I can't, the better the decision they'll be able to make. I want my audience to absolutely love buying from me, so I use a combination of visual brand elements and confident messaging to ensure they feel really seen and well supported at all stages of the process.

It's important that your brand has a rock-solid identity that looks and feels consistent across your website, social media, tone and style. This is where it's important to build a brand identity with intention and that's built on more than colours and fonts you like.

A good brand is instantly recognizable as your own, reflects your personality and talks to the people you want to call in. It knows what it is and what it is not. Without this clarity, the experience can look muddled and confusing, which makes it harder to attract the right clients.'

 **Helen's top tip**

Less is more! A couple of well-chosen fonts and colours can go a long way to create a cohesive look. Keep it simple and consistent – when your brand elements are uncluttered, they have more impact. Pair with a strong message throughout the stages of the decision maker's journey.

Find Helen on Instagram @mum_folk or at her website www.mumfolk.com for a whole host of branding, strategy and positioning wisdom.

# Now it's your turn!

## To be easy to buy from

Map out the journey you want your audience to take from first meet to making a decision. What are the key steps you want your audience to take along the way? How can you build connection and make each stage a dream for them in the process?

For example, your journey could look something like:

- Regular opportunities to hear you speak about why your business exists.
- Easy access to what people can expect in your world.
- Showcasing understanding of what your customers need and how you help solve their problems specifically.
- Plentiful examples of people you have worked with and stories demonstrating how you were able to create a desired result.
- Signposting opportunities to liaise with you to make decisions about working with you.

When you have the steps mapped out, look at how easy it is for potential clients to see content that verifies each stage and makes it easy to progress. For example, you might look to create blog posts, offer useful resources and have conversations about topics that showcase your opinions on topics relevant to your clients. Asking existing and past clients for feedback is a brilliant way to make improvements to your process.

1. Consider your last three online purchases. What helped you to buy – was it a feeling or a logical reason in the first instance? What particular elements appealed? Consider the branding elements, how clear you felt, what compelled you to buy when you did, and how long it took you to walk the journey from discovering the product to buying it. Did you buy on the first go, or did you receive multiple nudges at different times? Are you replicating these steps in your own sales process? If not, what can you add in to include the things that help you?

2. Looking at your own latest clients – do you know the reasons they decided to work with you? If not, ask them! Are there any commonalities or patterns?

3. When you think about the people you're creating for, what are the things they want? What do they crave having more of? What are they looking to feel better about, improve on or do more quickly? List out the things you can help with and start to notice ways in which your products can be positioned as specific solutions.

## Chapter recap

- Understanding how your buyer makes decisions is key to success. The easier you can make it to buy from you, the more sales you will make. Lead your buyer through a well thought-out process. Provide opportunity for emotional connection first, then follow up with logic.

- Small businesses have a unique opportunity to create really personal and well thought-out buying experiences and to use simple, consistent branding elements to build brand identity and connection.

- Selling is not about convincing someone to buy something they don't want – you are only looking for the people who *do* want what you have to offer.

- Not everyone is your ideal client and you are not everyone's ideal solution, and that's a good thing!

Now you understand buyer behaviour and how decisions are made, I think it's time we took a deeper dive into being a perfect solution for clients. Let's double down on what you've learned here by putting it all into words in Chapter 6.

# Chapter 6

# Solid sales foundations

*Trying to be like other people is not only draining, it's also really boring.*

(Ami Robertson, brand
photographer and coach)

Want to know what you can learn about business from bodybuilder turned action-hero turned politician Arnold Schwarzenegger? Well I'm going to tell you.

In his three-part Netflix documentary, which I just so happened to be watching last night, he shared a story about filming the sequel to Terminator. For context, in the late eighties/ early nineties, Arnie was the number one box office star in the world. That's after he won Mr Universe at 20 and became one of the biggest bodybuilders in the world, and before he turned his hand to politics and became Governor of California.

So, on the set of *Terminator 2: Judgement Day*, he was asked by Director James Cameron to impart some wisdom to the younger cast members to help make the movie a success. This is what he said:

*Half of the job is performing the film and half of the job is promoting the film. As an actor you have to be personally involved in talking about the film and to tell people why they should go out and watch it. It is not someone else's job to sell your thing, you have to sell it. Whatever you do in life, you have to sell it.*

On that note, I could end the book right here! The numbers certainly back him up: *Terminator 2* didn't make US$50 million like the original film. It became the highest grossing movie of 1991, bringing in US$520 million worldwide.[1]

Arnie knows what he's doing when it comes to selling. And doing it has amassed him a fortune of over US$400 million along the way.

If a lad from a tiny town in Austria and with barely any English can decide to move countries, turn his hand to body-building, become a world-famous actor and then move on to politics, I reckon that means you and I can spend a few minutes a day talking about our products on the internet from the comfort of our own homes, don't you? (I can honestly say I didn't know I was going to be delving into the eighties action movie genre when I set out to write this chapter, and yet here we are. Life is full of surprises.)

Take away: the energy you spend creating – whether that's blockbuster films, beautiful hand-crafted garments or online courses – it's only half the job. The other half is ensuring you are telling people why they should buy what you've made. If every creative, artist and business owner did this, the income generated would be huge.

In a recent poll of 1,000 small business owners in the UK, over 90% said they felt invisible on social media.[2] Forty per cent of business owners in the UK don't know how to advertise what they do. Six out of ten don't use social media at all. Half of those polled felt they would make more sales if they did.[3]

The message is clear: the more comfortable you can be taking small visibility actions each day, the easier it is for clients to buy from you and the more money you will make.

---

[1] www.goldenglobes.com/articles/how-arnold-schwarzenegger-came-baaack-terminator-2

[2] https://holly.co/campaign-shop-independent-2023/

[3] www.independent.co.uk/news/business/uk-businesses-social-media-poll-b1852747.html

**Reasons to be more visible**
- It helps more clients find and get to know you more easily.
- Sharing your unique opinions builds connection faster.
- It establishes you as a go-to expert.
- It makes sure you are positioning yourself as the solution to a specific known need.
- It educates your audience on how you can help them.
- It shows your clients you care about their overall experience.

Visibility expert Vicki Knights shares five tips to getting started with being visible online:

### Remember why you're doing this

When you're about to show up in your business in some way it can be scary, from the first time you share a photo of yourself on Instagram to pitching yourself as a guest on a podcast. You might start telling yourself that no one really wants to hear what you have to say, or what if no one engages with it (or the opposite, what if it goes viral?!)

When this happens, bring the focus back to why you started your business in the first place. Why do you do what you do? Think about who you are trying to help and what positive difference you want to make in the world. When you reconnect with your purpose, it makes being visible feel that much easier. You're not going to be able to make that positive impact by hiding. So just think about all of the people that you might be able to help by posting that photo, sharing that idea or appearing on that podcast.

## Get clear on your personal brand

There are many pieces that make up your personal brand – your values, purpose, strengths, skills, interests, personality, style and more. When you have clarity around this, getting visible becomes much easier. Without brand clarity, you'll find yourself fumbling around hoping something will work. Once you get really clear on your personal brand, everything falls into place and your marketing becomes so much easier.

Jeff Bezos once said, 'Your personal brand is what people say about you when you're not in the room'. Sounds a bit terrifying doesn't it? The brilliant thing about crafting your personal brand is that you can influence what they are saying about you!

## Don't be someone you're not

It's easy to think that you need to show up in a certain way to grow your business. But being something you're not can actually harm your business. People can smell inauthenticity a mile away. When you show yourself authentically and in a way that makes you feel good – it shows. Your clients will be drawn to you and your brand will stand out because you were yourself.

## Showing up is not showing off!

When you're about to post something online and annoying voices come in telling you people will judge you, try this reframe in your head.

### It's not about you, it's about them

You started your business because you want to help people and make a positive difference. *That's* why you're getting visible. You get to do it however feels right for you, so take it one step at a time. This is about reaching more people so that you can make a positive difference in their lives. Doesn't that feel better?

### The more you do it the easier it gets!

The first time you do anything, it's always a little nerve-racking. We're all at different stages of our visibility journey. For you perhaps even adding a photo of yourself to your 'about me' page is out of your comfort zone. Or perhaps you've been showing your face for a while but you haven't yet had the courage to try talking to camera. Whatever the next step is for you to become more visible in your business, please know that it does get easier. The second time you do it will be less scary and then by the tenth time it will feel like second nature. Just take the next step for you and know that visibility gets easier with every (baby) step that you take.

Vicki Knights is a visibility and personal brand strategist and photographer who has really nailed the art of weaving personal and professional through her content. I really recommend checking out Vicki for inspiration on how to show up and be relatable by being yourself. You can find her on Instagram @vickiknights.branding or via her website www.vickiknights.co.uk.

# Strategy foundations

Ninety-nine times out of a hundred, when a client comes to me with slow sales, the problem is that it isn't easy to find, it doesn't have a clearly spelled out purpose or it simply isn't being talked about by the creator.

An effective sales strategy is rock solid in the following three areas: the product you're selling, what it does for people, and how easy it is to find. These are your sales simplifiers, the things you need to have clear in your mind before active selling commences, so let's walk through them one by one.

# The product

## Ensuring what you're selling is desirable to the people you want to buy it

As business owners, one of the most exciting decisions we get to make is arriving at the suite of products or services we're going to actually sell. On some days, that's a real gift: infinite possibility! Choices for days! No end to the direction you can grow into! On a less good day, it can be overwhelming and impossible to know where to even start.

Getting your services just how you want them is often the result of weeks' (or even months') worth of work. No wonder, then, that it feels so completely crushing when you finally announce something is ready to buy, and nobody actually does.

This deflating situation is almost always the result of the offer not being presented with enough specificity around who it's for, what it does or why you made it. We know from Chapter 4 that leading with a solution to the problem is the key to both.

## Be the solution

The more sure your buyer can be that what you're selling is of value to them, the easier it will be for them to decide whether to buy it or not. Knowing how to create and package up your offers that speak to a certain segment of your audience is the difference between creating a service that sells versus creating a service that sits on your website gathering dust.

The first thing to work on is how to package up some of your knowledge or skill into a product that has a very specific type of buyer in mind. What to put in, what to leave out and where to draw the line.

If you want easy sales you need to create offers that people want to buy. You have to be clear about what's in it for the buyer. And you have to be seen so that those people can buy from you.

## Be specific

In my experience, by the time most people set up a business they have gathered a heck of a lot of experience, information and knowledge on a variety of different topics. They know a lot of things that could help a lot of people. And when this is the case, it can be tempting to leave things open so that a range of different clients come in. But when it comes to selling things on the internet, putting our hand up for everything we know how to do is a false friend.

In a physical shop, when a customer walks in, the first thing the shopkeeper says is, 'How can I help you?' In online selling, you have to *tell* people how you help them. The first thing your client wants to know is what you can do *for them*, and if this is buried or not immediately obvious, you'll lose their attention before you even had it.

## Know your niche

Being a generalist on the internet makes it really hard to stand out. The more specialized you present as, the easier it will be to stand out.

If you think about it, it's pretty obvious that it's easier to make a name for yourself in one area than becoming known as an expert in lots of things (even though you might perfectly well have multiple strings to your bow). It's going to take less time and energy to be known for one thing than trying to be known as the leading expert in *all of the things*. Now, this is not to say that your business will only ever be about one isolated thing, but it does help from a marketing perspective if people can easily see one thing you are able to help them with.

Online, if you can't appeal to one group of people, you won't appeal to any people. So, master one area first, then branch out from there if you want to. A clearly defined niche will make it a heck of a lot easier to be noticed by the people you want to work with, right from day one, and that's a tool worth having in my book, at least in the beginning. Therefore, from an efficiency perspective, it's a good idea to speak about what you're selling in terms of a niche. This is especially true if you want to hit consistent sales quickly. If your niche isn't clear, your ideal client can't self-identify and the segment of the market you most want to work with doesn't know you're talking to them.

Does making a name for yourself in a certain niche constrict your business? No. Does having an ownable niche make it easier for clients to find you and work with you? Yes. Does it mean you need to stay in that niche forever and never do anything else? No.

The biggest benefit of knowing your niche is that it makes it much easier for the people in your audience to feel seen and spoken to, and to see that your skills in this guise have an application that is relevant for them.

## Articulate the value

As we saw in Chapter 5, everyone has things they want to get better at, have more of, spend less time on, feel happier about… and these are constantly evolving. From keeping fit to eating for energy, to preparing for a certain life stage (having a baby, menopause, retirement) to building a garden shed and everything in between… the list is endless!

Our job when creating products and services is to ensure we are facilitating the desires of our audience of potential buyers, and presenting solutions that talk specifically to them. The way you package up your knowledge needs to relate to a certain type of buyer, with a certain type of problem or situation that they are craving help with and have a clear and specific transformation it enables.

In order to buy something, your ideal client needs to immediately know what's in it for them. Nobody will buy something they don't see the value in. Let's ensure what you're selling shines like an irresistible beacon to the people you made it for. Getting this right means the decision to make about whether to buy it is very simple: it's either relevant and required or it isn't. If they don't understand the value, they don't understand what the reason is to buy it.

## Who is the offer for?

- Who are you selling it to and what is the known problem or situation that this person has?
- What specifically do people come to you for?
- What result are you really good at getting for people?

## What does it do?

- All irresistible offers create change or feed an aspiration.
- What can the person who buys it reasonably expect to be different afterwards?
- What will the overall experience be like?
- How would you describe your style of delivery or working?

## What specific, known problem does it solve?

- Why did you create it and what is the result you intend for the people who purchase this?
- What will be easier afterwards, what will the buyer gain?
- What specifically do people desire that this service or product makes easier?

People buy change, not products or services, so in order to pique your buyer's interest, your offer must be created around a change that is desired by your ideal client. Get crystal clear on these elements and your audience will find it easier to connect with your offers from the get-go.

# The positioning

### Ensure you're telling people what it does for them, so they don't have to figure it out alone

One of the most often overlooked tools in your sales toolkit is potent messaging. In business you are required to communicate your message daily, in multiple different ways, and so it's crucial that what you're saying activates the right people to move instead of getting lost in translation or leaving people scratching their heads.

The way you talk about your products determines how effective your visibility effort will be: if your message is unclear, your visibility will fall flat because nobody will know what on earth you're talking about. Strong messaging positions what you do as highly relevant. It is how you attract clients and get your work into the hands of the people who want it. The words you use matter just as much as the product or service itself, because if you can't capture the attention and imagination of your audience, nobody will decide to buy it. The more precise you can be, the more impact you will have.

Your ideal client doesn't have time for woolly, fluffy or self-indulgent communication. They don't care as much about what's in it for you, they care about what's in it for them. This shift in perspective is important, because a lot of the time, business owners overly qualify why they have created something, without telling their audience why that matters.

So, kick things off with what's in it for your client and you'll give yourself the best possible chance of success. When messaging is done well, the sales journey is straightforward because demand has been established upfront.

| Vague message that focuses on creator | Clear message that focuses on client |
| --- | --- |
| 'I made this product to bring together my extensive research into UK motorways spanning 15 years.' | 'I made this product to stop you getting lost on car journeys.' |
| 'My latest collection embodies my current evolution, brings in elements of all my idols and reflects my recent travels in South East Asia and Japan.' | 'My latest collection is colourful, it's flattering, it's ethically produced and I made it for busy women to feel fabulous in, everywhere from the school run to weekends of fun.' |

| 'In this course I share my skills as a writer.' | 'In this course I will teach you how to write your first novel, from approaching publishers, to outlining the book structure, to chapter do's and don'ts. You will learn everything you need to turn your idea into the finished book manuscript.' |
| --- | --- |

Get your messaging right and clients will buy into what you're selling on their own: this is attraction marketing at its best. Wishy washy messaging makes the sales process much harder because it doesn't captivate your audience or make them want to know more.

An incomplete or fluffy message can partially explain why many of the sales stereotypes about pushy selling that we explored in Part I exist in the first place. If messaging isn't well thought-out enough to do its job of attracting clients naturally, it leaves a bigger job to do on the backend to enable a sale to happen. Therefore, if you want to create ease and flow with sales *it's so important* that you let your messaging do the work of allowing your ideal client to self-identify for you.

Your messaging is the thing that shrinks the amount of time it takes to decide to work with you. Effective messaging is every bit worth pursuing as it simplifies the sales process, is of genuine service to your clients and vastly speeds up the amount of time it takes someone to buy from you. It is the first opportunity people get to understand what your business is about. As well as being the driving force behind your sales strategy, it represents you in various locations online and in real life too. It's not freezing up when asked 'what do you do' at a networking event. It's having an elevator pitch that hits the spot. It's articulating how your services effect change for people. It's in your lead generation. It's everywhere, including:

- the homepage of your website;
- your social media bio;

- what you say at networking events;
- how you describe your business to friends and family;
- the way you position your products to your audience.

When I first started out as a photographer, I found editing on my own all week a big adjustment from working in a busy trading floor. So, I'd spend a lot of time at networking events to socialize and make friends. Turns out they're also a great place for picking up new business too!

**Networking tip**

Each time someone asks you what you do, what they're really asking is: what can you do for *me*. So, instead of answering literally, create a response that tells the person asking a little bit more. Tell them the ultimate benefit of working with you, share who most of your clients are and why they come to you. To make this easier, a good rule of thumb is to follow the 'who, what, why' approach.

- *Who* is it for?
- *What* does it do for them?
- *Why* should they care?

To be completely clear: Don't just say what you do and announce your job title – attach it to a certain type of client with a specific issue or goal. This micro-upgrade enables the person you're talking to to see past your job title and get straight to considering whether you have something they need right now. In the few seconds you've got to make an impact, this maximizes the opportunity.

Let's look at the example of a wedding photographer. Even though there are lots of other types of photography, wedding photography is still a huge niche. What makes one couple happy will have another couple recoil in horror, so it's important you know how to stand out to those who are best aligned with your skillset.

What are your favourite type of clients or weddings like? Maybe you're a wedding photographer for fun-loving couples who care more about the party than the traditional details. Perhaps your speciality is amazing dance floor shots. Maybe you focus on capturing the emotion of the day. Whatever your favourite aspects are, don't forget to tell people!

*Who* is it for?
Are you for non-traditional couples, dance floor-focused couples, are country barn weddings your thing ... or something else?

*What* does it do for them?
Perhaps you deliver a beautiful, timeless set of photos that captures memories from the day that will last a lifetime. Maybe your focus is on capturing important family members throughout the day. Or is it that you know how to blend in easily with friends and family alike?

*Why* should they care?
Are you good at relaxing camera-shy couples? Do you geek out over dance floor shots? Is your superpower gathering big groups and getting them in position at superspeed? Are you a winter wedding specialist who can take flattering photos even in low-light venues?

Whatever industry you work in, think about what makes you the right fit for a certain buyer and shift the way you talk so that the focus is more on them and what they stand to gain, than you and your expertise.

# The promotion

## Ensure your clients can easily find you by getting your message seen

Being visible is how you get your products in front of the right people. It's taking your carefully constructed solution and your marvellous message and putting it out into spaces where you know your ideal clients will actually see it. This could be a variety of online and real-life locations, from social media platforms, networking spaces, your website, online communities, podcasts… in fact, there have never been more places or ways to shine a light on what you do and find more clients!

Only a few years ago, the only practical ways to build visibility were to get a website, have business cards to hand out at networking events and print out pamphlets to distribute locally. Now, in just a few clicks you can reach ideal clients all over the globe, for free, straight from your phone. Mind blowing but brilliant, right?

Now that business owners can access such a wide-ranging client base at the touch of a button, the need for specificity to cut through the noise is more important than ever. This is what's going to stand you head and shoulders above the rest and enable your client to see *you* as the person they want to work with.

---

Be visible. showing up with a clear message is one of the best ways you can help your audience see what's available to them. The more visible you are, the easier it is to get to know you and your products.

---

### Ami Robertson on … finding ease being visible online

Ami Robertson of The Wolf and the Wild Thing is a brand photographer who supports business owners on their journey to visibility confidence by helping them create photos that reflect who they really are, so that they feel really confident about sharing them. I am probably one of the hardest people to photograph, and they nailed it (as shown on the cover of this book). I asked them to share some of their wisdom and personal insight about how to feel more comfortable showing up, and this is what they said:

'I found showing up online hard at first – low self-esteem and this idea that it had to be done in a certain way playing their parts. As soon as I realized that I didn't need to be perfect I felt a lot more free, and my confidence grew from there.

As an autistic person with confidence issues, it took me a while to really step into my power. That was when things shifted, alongside mastering my style. Being clear about why I want to help people love their photos made a big difference as well.

I use social media to show my audience who I am and what I stand for, and to nurture relationships from there. For me photography is incredibly empowering as a way to take up space: my clients come to me to develop their confidence around being seen. I want to do my part in making sure the online space is more diverse and better represented, so the more women and anyone else who isn't a cis/het/white/able-bodied man that I can help show up and feel good about doing that, the better.

About a third of my work comes from social media, with the rest coming from other marketing efforts, repeat clients and referrals. It wasn't until I became more consistent and regularly showed up that things shifted. Also setting clear goals and learning how to properly run a business, especially around money.'

 **Ami's top tips**

Feeling overwhelmed is the biggest killer of small businesses, so create a strategy that can be easily maintained. My best marketing tactics are SEO, networking and social media so I make sure I focus on them. Be yourself! Trying to be like other people is not only draining long term, it's also really boring in a crowded space. I find socials incredibly dull a lot of the time because of its lack of authenticity and the amount of people just trying to be like everyone else. You stand out when you take up space as yourself. Also, remember that things take time. Nothing is going to work straight away, so don't give up.'

Follow Ami on Instagram @thewolfandthewildthing or head to their website www.thewolfandthewildthing.com for a whole host of beautiful brand photos that will give you a surge of inspiration for your own!

# Now it's your turn!

## To be visible and tell people what you can do for them

Put together a sentence that positions what you're selling in terms of what you can do for people. Use the 'who, what, why' approach to craft this:

- Who is the ideal client for what you're selling? Who do you want to buy it?
- What do they need help with right now? What solution are you offering?
- Why should they care about your product? What does it do for them?

And, for a bonus point, how do you deliver on this specific want/need?

A useful way to get started is to write out the following positioning sentence: 'I help [ideal client] with [challenge they are experiencing] so that they can [achieve specific desired outcome or result]'.

You don't have to stick to this exact sentence if you don't want to. Use it as a helpful way to start thinking about talking in terms of what you do for other people and shift the perspective away from you.

When you have your positioning statement clear you'll find it so much easier to show up and to know what to talk about. To make it even easier to get visible, why not think about getting some new headshots that make you feel really confident?

## Chapter recap

- If every business owner matched the time they spent creating products to sell with promoting them, the impact on their rate of growth and income would be enormous. As Arnie said: half the job is making the film and half the job is promoting the film! Showing up and talking about what you do is just as important as creating products to sell.
- There are three foundational elements to selling. Having a product that solves a problem, a message that communicates what it does for clients, and a commitment to showing up and advocating for the product.
- Being visible is more about your clients than it is about you. Shift the perspective and communicate more what it is about your products that can help them, and less what your products do for you.

That's the foundations set, now let's put them into a step-by-step strategy. Onwards to Chapter 7 for the full breakdown of the four stages in the process.

# Chapter 7

# Your sales strategy step by step

*My sales plan gave me confidence and doubled my sales.*
(Lucie Sheridan, live portrait artist)

Once, I got lost driving back from Bristol, where my boyfriend at the time was at uni. Even though I'd taken the trip several times before, I ended up, not, as I'd hoped, home in Hertfordshire but instead, in the terminal 3 car park at Heathrow Airport. It was before the digital era, so I was sans sat nav and the most useful thing my Nokia mobile phone had on it was the ever so of its time game: Snake. So, I had to guess my way home, and it took five hours longer than it should have done. It was harrowing stuff.

I wasn't blessed with even the remotest sense of direction. It's maddening. Even when I definitely *should* know my way in a familiar area, I still regularly get lost and go the wrong way. So I am one of those people who will never tell you to figure it out as you go. I know the heavy expense of a wrong turn, I feel it viscerally and often wonder, if I added up the amount of time I've spent 'lost', how many years of my life I'd get back.

Think about it: if you wanted to drive up to Scotland for the first time, you probably wouldn't just get into the car with no clue as to the route, start driving around and see where you ended up (this actually sends shivers down my spine, just thinking about it). No, instead, you'd pop the postcode into sat nav and let the wonders of modern technology lead the way.

Moral of the story: if you want to get somewhere specific, you need a roadmap.

A common mis-step business owners make is to throw themselves into social media before mapping out the sales plan. This is not only time consuming, but also a sure-fire way to end up feeling fed up. Yes, being visible is important, but it only works if it's used to support a sales plan: otherwise, you run the risk of the time you invest in showing up online falling flat: not helping your buyer, not helping your bottom line, not leading to sales.

Before we go charging onto social media, we need to be clear of its role in our business, that is, how we will use it. Your sales plan controls everything from your marketing activity to the way you show up to share information online, the steps in your process, how you qualify your leads, the way you lead discovery calls, the experience you give your clients before they're paying clients, how you help them make decisions.

Right now, your sales process might be more reactive than proactive. Reactive sales strategies rely on waiting for word of mouth or referrals, and then sitting on your hands or taking random action while you wait and wish for this to happen. These strategies often result in sporadic periods of sales success, followed by a lull.

Proactive sales strategies are about understanding what the steps are that you need to take to control the volume of sales coming into your business, so that you are in control of how many clients you bring in each month. Having a map to follow to attract clients takes away your stress and keeps you on the right path.

Your sales process removes procrastination, curbs feeling overwhelmed, streamlines your action, simplifies the client experience and gets you out of creation mode and into *doing* mode.

Your sales strategy will help you:

- if you're time poor or like to be efficient;
- if you find selling overwhelming or something you procrastinate over;

- if you want more clients in a more streamlined way;
- to connect what you're selling with the people who'd like to buy it;
- to ensure you don't just get more clients, but more of the right clients;
- to provide a high standard of experience and show your audience you care.

Let's say you're looking to sign ten new clients this month. Your sales plan lays out the specific actions you need to take that will make this happen, and makes sure nothing gets missed out.

Depending on your business model, there may be five to ten actions that, when done in an orderly way, will help somebody come into your world, get to know you and your products, feel confident about whether what you're doing is something they desire, and then make a decision to pay for it.

First, you'll need to make sure you have a large enough pool of potential clients to speak to. Perhaps you're already confident that your audience contains a good number of people for whom your service is perfect – or maybe you'll need to include some additional visibility activity to create even more awareness for your services.

Next you need to create opportunities to have conversations with those people. How are the people in your audience able to get to know you and how well suited this service is for them? Are you sending emails to them? Is there somewhere online they can go to familiarize themselves with your work (your website, a blog, social media, YouTube?). If this information is readily available – how regularly are you sending people there?

Are you speaking about the path they should take frequently enough for them not to have to guess? Can you be sure people know what is available to them? Is it easy for those people to know what options they have to buy from you, and what the outcomes will be if they do? Are you talking about how they can take next steps? Are there clear calls to action at every juncture, from your website pages to what you say online? Your sales strategy is how you make sure all this happens seamlessly, in the right order, and to maximum benefit.

With a clear strategy, each action you take in the day to day running of your business has a specific purpose and you feel clear about how to grow. Your client has transparency at every stage.

Without one, you can feel like you're taking random action that isn't getting you the traction you are wishing for. Your audience often doesn't know where they should go next or how to progress as easily through your content.

---

**What does a good sales plan look like?**

✓ Attracts new people into your world regularly.
✓ Provides consistent nurturing content to prospective buyers at all stages.
✓ Ensures your client has a clear route to buy.
✓ Increases the opportunities to make a sale.
✓ Presents the benefits of buying in a straightforward way.
✓ Instils confidence, clarity and connection.
✓ Elevates the standard of experience your clients receive.
✓ Makes it easy for you to track what's working.
✓ Makes it simple to identify problems or gaps and know how to fix them.
✓ Stops you feeling like you 'should' be doing more.
✓ Removes the tasks that are keeping you busy but aren't providing a return on your time.

---

A well thought-out plan puts advance thought behind the way new people are able to find you, what their first experience of you is like, and how they can then get to know more. There will be multiple touchpoints in your process that facilitate the way new people get to know you, how they can find out about what you offer, and the ease with which they can progress to paying customer if they would like.

These are the key steps that are required in your sales plan to help your audience transition from first finding you, to being familiar enough with your work to making a decision to buy – Relevance, Audience Nurturing, Conversations and Experience. When all these phases work together, consistent sales become straightforward.

## The 'Race' to consistent sales

Relevance: In this phase you use visibility activity to let people know you have something to sell that is highly valuable to a specific group of people.

Audience nurturing: In this phase your focus is to allow clients to become familiar with you and your work. You do this via content that nurtures your audience and allows them to get to know you at their own pace. Having a strategy around this is how you take people from feeling like you're a perfect stranger to being familiar with your business, your personality and how both are a match for them.

Conversations: In this phase your priority is to establish suitability and instil your clients with confidence in you and your products.

Experience: In the final phase your priority is to deliver excellent standards of care. Providing decision support and a way to answer questions so that your client can complete the process with conviction.

Let's look at each stage and build each one out step by step.

## Stage one: Relevance

In this phase you use strategic visibility activity to introduce new people to the value inside your products and offers. Do this by getting in front of new audiences and talking about your product in terms of them, not you. The problem isn't whether your buyers exist. It's whether they can find you.

## Getting your business seen

There are various ways to get your business seen. You can make your way to your nearest hill or market square and wave your arms around while shouting about what you can do for people until they start paying attention. (I read somewhere that this is how Joe Wicks, aka the Body Coach, started out – by trogging down to his local park every week, running PT sessions and getting word out there in his local community about the benefits of exercising on how you feel. What started as getting the word out locally grew and grew, and he now has a multi-million pound business and over 4.6 million followers on Instagram, so I'd say it worked out OK for him. It's a perfectly good strategy.)

If you don't like braving the elements and taking it on the chin when nobody rocks up in lycra to squat with you, there is (mercifully) an alternative option available to you. You can go online wearing garments as loose as you like. Instead of getting soggy day after day in your local park, through the gift of social media you can send out flares of relevance from the comfort of your home. You can send relevant emails to your community. You can share relevant snippets of info every day without leaving your desk if you don't want to. How marvellous.

## Lead with relevance

Communicating your relevance in the right places draws people to you in an altogether more leaned back way. It's like sending out invitations to a fabulous party – you post messages with intention, you wait, and before long, you start getting excited RSVPs landing on your doorstep.

Trying to sell something without showcasing relevance is like throwing a huge party and having nobody bothering to turn up on the night. It's awful! It's crushing! It's a giant ruddy disappointment.

If you want your party (business) to be packed with fun-loving revellers who are going to have the best time they've had in ages, you need to be clear on who your dream guests are and what a great night out looks like for them. Give them a clear reason to come. They are busy. They get lots of invitations to things. Blow everything else that's happening on that night out of the water – make sure your guests know to save the date because you've made it easy for them to see it was made for them. Maybe you know their dream venue – and secured it. Nailed the playlist and locked in their favourite DJs to play on the night. You read the room and how long it's been since they danced the night away, and you're making a pledge to put that right.

The easiest way to immediately appeal, get attention and build an army of enthusiastic buyers is to lead with relevance. The easier you can make it for those people to see *why* your product is relevant to them, the more sales you will make. Relevance is nothing to do with you and everything to do with your client, as we saw in Chapter 6. People only buy things that benefit *them*. So always showcase your product as something they are actually looking for.

1. *Who is your ideal guest for the party (client for this product)?*
Each product or service you offer will likely have a slightly different target client. Knowing exactly who you want to come to the party and tailoring your message to create their dream night is how you crank up the enthusiasm and value awareness for what you're doing.

When I tell people I'm throwing a party, the first thing they're going to want to know is what *kind* of party it will be. Will it be a dinner party, a kids' party, a dancing party, a garden party? Is it a daytime thing, a late-night thing, an intimate gathering or a stonking great festival type bonanza?

If the overall vibe of this party is dancing to the best tunes from the nineties, I need to share that loud so that lovers of heavy metal bands know not to come. Likewise, if I'm having a dinner party for a few friends – I need to spread the word about the vibe and the food I'll be serving up. The more I tailor this to the people I want to be there, the more I help the people I'm inviting decide if it's up their street or not. The very same thing is true for your business: who is your ideal client – who do you really want to be there?

### 2. *What do they need your help with right now?*

Present each service or product as a solution to a specific problem, rather than a general 'nice to have' so that more of your audience can understand how your products can be applied to their lives. Your offer will appeal and stand out a whole lot more if it has a direct outcome. It is the initial sign-post that its ideal buyer will see. Without pinning this down, your offer will float about in the ether, unable to connect with the people it can help.

### 3. *How does your product or service deliver on a specific need?*

Consider your guestlist: what would make this experience *really* special for them? Sticking with the party analogy for now:

- Are they craving an opportunity to let their hair down?
- Have they been missing the dancing opportunities that were such a big part of previous life stages?
- Perhaps they no longer go dancing because there isn't anything that caters for people who don't drink or want to stay out late?

In your business, consider the following:

- If you could sell your products to absolutely anyone, who would it be and why?
- List all the ways your expertise, products and services could help that person with their specific situation, aspiration or thing they want to do better. How do they feel?
- What does the person you're creating for already know about your topic?
- What is available in your space already and how are you similar/different?

Tethering your wares to a particular result, aspiration or desired outcome rather than leaving it to assumption ensures your potential buyer has at least one direct use for what you're selling to refer to. Without you spelling it out for them, you run the risk that your audience can't see how your skills can help them, and relevance is not established.

No relevance, no interest: as we discussed in Chapter 6, if people can't instantly see what your offer can do for them, they're going to someone else's party.

*Top tip: Make sure your product or service is highly relevant and responds directly to a need you know your audience is craving.*

Get this right and you'll attract a merry band. Get it wrong and nobody will RSVP. Without the relevance, for the people online who are searching for the exact type of occasion you're planning, it's like looking for a needle in a haystack. Not. Going. To. Happen. Think about it: if I invited you to my party and gave you absolutely zero details about what kind of party it was, where it was, whether it was to your tastes, would you come?

## The sweet spot: strategic visibility + relevant messaging

OK, so your guest list is written out and you know who you're inviting to the party of the century. Now what?

Next, it's time to make sure you're being seen by the people on that list and that they are in your audience. It's time to create demand and drive traffic to what you're selling. Calling in an audience of people who are the perfect fit for your offer is the part that most businesses under-do and then wonder why they aren't making more sales.

Most businesses don't have a problem creating products and services. Most have a problem getting customers to know about them and buy them. That's why selling and visibility are so linked. This is why Arnie got it so right (head back to Chapter 6 if you don't know what I'm on about).

It doesn't matter how well you're sharing relevant value, or how much standing on a hill in a high-vis vest you're doing – if you are talking to people who don't value the thing you're selling, they aren't going to buy it. So it's not *only* visibility that matters, it's being strategic about where you're showing up, and what you're saying when you're there.

Your ideal client is not only the person who has the problem you're looking to solve, but also the person who has this problem *and is out there looking to fix it right now*. The way that we call *those* people in and build the right audience is via messaging: what we say in the content we create online. By making sure the marketing we put out speaks only to them, we are able to build an audience of the right buyers *and* generate leads for our business. So the combination of relevant marketing and relevant visibility action is the sweet spot.

Focus on up to three 'new' places each month in addition to nurturing your existing community. This ensures you are always making it easy for new people to find you, as well as giving them relevant, fresh content when they do. Pick from the list of relevance-building visibility activities to focus on to get your business in front of new ideal clients:

- Network in person and via online events.
- Use local advertising in your area.
- Make new connections through people in your existing community.
- Be present and of service in Facebook groups, e.g. local business groups.
- Guest blog posts for business owners that share similar ideal clients to you.
- Be interviewed on other people's podcasts, where the audience is a match for your products.

I have found over the years that there is no one 'magic source' when it comes to finding new audience members. You can speak on a podcast with a huge following and have it make zero difference in terms of people coming to find you afterwards. Equally, you can be mentioned in a small, niche email newsletter that has really engaged subscribers and find a hundred new signups to your email list or social media following as a result. You can never predict what will happen, so my advice is to do your part in showing up, and enjoy it!

## Marketing your relevance

Your marketing activity carries your relevance into the world. It is how you share messages and pieces of information that attract more of the right clients. This is everything, from the copy on your website to what you say at networking events, the content you put onto social media, the things you say on your blog, the emails you send, the podcast episodes you create… if its goal is to call in the right clients, it's marketing.

The sales process then takes your potential client through a nurturing process, so that your new guest can familiarize themselves with your business and products in a way that ultimately makes it easy for them to decide whether to make a purchase.

Your sales system is made up of both marketing activity, which establishes relevance, gets the attention of ideal clients and brings new eyes to your business, and sales activity, which are the steps in the customer journey, escorting people to their decision-making destination.

Marketing is the relevance and visibility action you take that gets people's attention and brings them into your world. It combines what you say (your messaging) with where you are visible. Instead of choosing pushy selling styles (no thank you) we focus on attraction marketing, clear messaging and making ourselves available for conversations to bring in leads and sign new clients. This is the sales process in action.

## Relevance: summary

A sales process begins when you have the attention of ideal clients. Look at your audience right now – does it have a good number of people in it who love the kind of party you're throwing? If not, stay here in stage one of the process, marketing your business, getting strategically visible so that you're getting in front of the right pairs of eyes for what you're selling, and building relevance so that more people know about your party and how they can get involved. You'll know it's working when your audience is growing.

| Stage purpose: relevance | Build awareness that you exist. Bring new people into your world by strategic visibility activity. Get visible in front of new audiences, connect new people with your business, build awareness for your products and ensure you are communicating the relevance. |
|---|---|
| Actions to take in this stage | Visibility activities that are external to your existing audience, for example, networking, collaborations, guest blogging or providing content for someone else's newsletter, podcast interviews, and so on. |
| How you know it's working | Seeing your audience grow: new followers to your page, your email, your Facebook group or wherever you track your numbers. |
| How you know it's not working and what to do about it | Your visibility endeavours are not capturing attention or converting to new followers or audience members. It could be that relevance is not being established, the people you are in front of are not the right people, or that you are not visible enough yet. |

# Stage two: Audience nurturing

Once your visibility is working and the marketing activity is attracting new people to you, the next step is to allow your new arrivals to get to know you and your business. Warming up or nurturing your audience is how we do this. It is too soon to sell to someone when they have just arrived – first they need time and space to explore and research more about you and what you have to offer. They need emotional connection, they need context and they need time to understand what your business is all about.

The goal is to build emotional connection and create opportunities for meaningful conversations about working together, by moving people through a really intentional pathway that allows them to familiarize themselves with your business and your work. At any given time, there will be people in your audience who are ready to buy, and those that aren't. Stage two is where we call forward the people who are looking for help *now*.

## Content creation and the nurture phase

Nurturing is the way you allow people to get to know you, your values and the products you sell. This happens via the content you create. There are different content types for each stage of the journey.

The nurturing process takes your new guests from brand new into your world (strangers who have only just 'met you') to a place where they can be really familiar with your work, your business and your personality. Through the content you create and make available, your audience can take what they need and from here they can proceed to having meaningful conversations and making informed decisions that are right for them.

## The customer journey: from cold to warm to hot

### Cold audience

Your audience can be described as 'cold' when they are brand new to your world. Perhaps they saw you doing an interview with someone they knew, and decided to follow you online but apart from that know very little about you. They have just arrived and are curious to find out if they should stick around.

A cold audience is not ready to buy from you and won't be inspired to take action if you sell to them. First, what's required is headline information that speaks to their need and makes it obvious that you can help them.

A key way to help people progress from cold to warm is to focus on building connection. Do this by creating content that:

- identifies the problems you help your clients fix or improve;
- builds connection to you as a personal brand;
- deepens connection to their ability to access the future state they desire.

The goal of this phase is to introduce the theme your product or service helps with, to build connection with your audience, and to seed the options that are available. This helps your new guest feel clear about whether this is something they can identify with. If it is, they will want to stay long enough to know more detail.

**Key messages for phase one:**

- What is the specific problem or set of circumstances your business exists to help with?
- Why exactly is this an issue for your audience: how does it impact them?
- What are the benefits as you see them of taking action to resolve or move past this current state?

**Connection building content ideas for phase one:**

- Relevant statistics or key statements that bring the theme into sharp focus.
- What is your personal experience with this theme? Did you overcome the issue? How? Share relevant stories.

- Why are you passionate about this subject? What does solving the problem unlock or allow for you or your clients?
- What's your unique perspective on the wider impact of this problem existing, or the wider impact of reducing the problem?
- Share your knowledge: common things that hold people back, mistakes, reasons they haven't yet solved the issue.
- Intro post/recap what you're all about, what you love about your work and typical results.

If your audience is cold, you won't be getting much traction from the content you're putting out, enquiries happen rarely and you aren't getting regular sales. Spend more time creating content that makes it clear what your take is on the theme of your product or service. Are you explaining why the problem is such a big problem in your eyes? Are you sharing your own opinions on this and giving your audience your insights on this topic? Make sure you have something to say on the subject, and that you're saying it, as this helps people connect on a more personal level when you do.

## Warm audience

A warm audience interacts with your content and engages when you post content or send out emails. They already know the main topics you are an expert in, and the next phase is to deepen their understanding of what the outcomes, results or changes are that your products make happen. Now that they are clear on the context, they are ready to hear you talk more about specifically where your products can take them. Clues that you have warm people in your audience include starting to receive messages asking questions or requesting further information.

If phase one is to raise awareness of the problem or themes you can help your audience with, phase two is where you provide a specific solution to that problem, and talk about your service in terms of the beginning point and the end point. Explain what your product changes for people. Where exactly does it take them from and to? It's really important that you share where people can reasonably expect to finish, so that your audience can deepen their clarity around whether this is a fit for them.

**Key messages for phase two:**

- What is the transformation your product provides?
- What are the results you're really good at getting for people?
- Who is it for and who is it *not* for?

**Clarity building content for phase two:**

- A to B transformation: What is the exact start and end point?
- When is the right time for people to buy this product? Is it for beginners? Intermediate level? Advanced?
- What are the tangible and intangible benefits?
- Who exactly did you have in mind when you created this?
- Common pitfalls that take time if you don't know how to navigate and how this can help.
- Repeat what the problem is and how this solves that problem.
- Why people buy this and what they say about it.
- Share social proof and case studies.

**Hot audience**

The goal is to carry as many people through your nurturing content through to this phase, because when your audience is hot it means they are ready to take the next step to making a purchasing decision. This will often be done by booking a sales conversation with you.

Now that they are bought into the problem you're solving and the transformation you're pledging, it's time to go into more detail about what the product or overall experience will be like. This is the stage where people are ready to hear you talk about what's available – they want to be presented with their options and a clear route to buy.

Phase three is all about creating content that provides the full detail and information about what the experience will be like for those who say yes to working with you. The goal of this phase is to invite questions, be present for messages, provide the highest standard of care and make it as easy as possible for people to have conversations with you. Show up in full for your audience so that they are aware of what buying your products will be like.

**Key messages for phase three:**

- What will the experience be like?
- What's the intention you have for the people who buy this product?
- Repeat who exactly you made it for and what the intended result is.

When your audience is hot you'll know because they'll be asking for more in-depth conversations with you – requesting to jump on a call or tell them more about how they can work with you.

## Audience nurturing: summary

As you will be constantly welcoming new people into your world, there will be people at all stages of the customer journey in your audience at any one time. You can use the content you create to provide the key messages required for each phase.

**Phase one: problem awareness phase**
Show your clients the problem or starting point your work helps with.

**Phase two: provide clarity about the transformation**
Help your clients understand how the solution you have put
together works to effect change.

**Phase three: share detailed information about the product or
experience**
Help your clients get a feel for what buying from you looks like
and break down your product or service in greater detail.

| Stage purpose: audience nurturing | Build clarity, connection and confidence that leads to conversations.<br><br>To allow people to get to know you and familiarize themselves with your business and understand the outcomes of your products. |
|---|---|
| Actions to take in this stage | Delivery of key messages that nurture your audience and warm them up to your world. |
| How you know it's working | People will reach out and enquire about how to work with you, book conversations or want to find out more. |
| How you know it's not working and what to do about it | If your nurturing content is not converting to conversations or interest, you have a clarity or a messaging problem: your content is missing a piece and your audience is not easily moving from cold to warm to hot. Build out the clarity piece. |

# Stage three: Conversations

When clients are booking calls with you to discuss whether your products are right for them, your focus is to provide the best service you can. The goal is not to get the 'yes' but to help your client make the decision that's right for them at the right time.

The conversation is your opportunity to demonstrate the high standard of service you provide. The more you can deliver excellence before a sale, the easier it is for your client to feel certain about the type of experience they can reasonably expect after the sale. So, while sales conversations aren't for everyone – the clients that want them will really appreciate you making yourself available for them.

Conversations are by no means the only way to create sales for your business. There are lots of different ways to make a sale – what matters is that you have a mechanism for people to easily buy that works for you. For some business owners, a follow-up call after sending a proposal leads to the sale. For others, the whole sales process happens via links being shared and suitability being chatted about directly in Instagram. Whether you keep a list of 'warm leads' in your notebook that you follow up with, or you have an online process that works for you – the golden rule is to remember that closing sales is an active sport.

There will always be clients who buy without interacting with you personally, but in the main, getting a potential buyer through your sales process requires active participation on your side. *You* are the draw of your business, so be present and lead the process.

## Sales call framework

Sales calls are a brilliant opportunity to personally assess suitability for your products and services and to show your client their experience matters to you. I have found it helpful to use this framework that centres around *service*, not selling.

In order to assess whether your products are a good fit for your client, you first need to understand their current situation and obstacles. Knowledge is always better than assumption, so asking the right questions is key. Ask questions that will help you understand your client's existing struggles, timelines and goals. You need to understand the current stage they're at and specifically what they're aiming for, because this will be different for everyone.

The first three-quarters of your sales process is therefore about you asking the questions you need to know the answers to in order to assess suitability.

This is a step-by-step guide to leading sales conversations with integrity:

1. Introduction – understand why this person got in touch.
2. Research problem – what is going on for this person, what are they struggling with specifically? Was there a particular event that has led them to you?
3. Understand goals – where does your client want to go from here? What is the outcome they are looking to achieve?
4. Qualify – why do they need your help specifically – what with?

Before you can provide a meaningful solution, you first need to satisfy yourself that you understand the problem for this person. Stay here before proceeding and until you are able to establish whether you are someone who can help them, and how. I cannot stress enough how important it is that you do your due diligence and assess suitability before making any recommendations. Get the full scope of their problem before you provide a solution and always lead *with integrity*. Failing to pair up a need with a solution is what leaves so many people having suboptimal experiences on both sides.

Sales calls are about qualifying, providing your reassurance on suitability and then making invitations. Once you know their problems and where they want to go, you invite them to find out more about how you can help.

When you're sure they are the right fit for your solution:

1. Tell them why specifically you think you can help them and invite them to learn more about your proposed solution.
2. Close – proceed to next steps: proposal, purchase – what happens now? Let your prospect know what to expect from you, and when.

**Helpful hints for your next sales call:**

- Open by saying the purpose of the call is for you both to better understand whether you might be a good fit for each other.
- Be clear that the call is *not* about getting a sale, it's about providing due care and attention to the human being on the other end: finding out where they're at so you can share information that will help them make an informed decision.
- Lead the conversation by asking the questions that will unlock the information you need to be able to help.
- Research the problem and uncover the aspirations of your client. What are they working on and how quickly are they hoping to get there?
- Why do they need your help, and can you actually give them what they need?
- If they are the right fit and you can help them, invite them to learn more about what working with you will look like.
- Set the scene and be specific about what you will work through together and what will be different at the end.
- What happens next? Tell them if you'll send a summary note, ask them if they have any questions and be clear about how they can proceed when they have made their decision.

Leading calls this way ensures you are providing a tailored service that's relevant for your clients. It shows you care about the experience they will have with you to tell them about it, and allows them to get a feel for how you'll fit together, which is so important especially for people who might have had their fingers burnt in the past and be feeling nervous about investing. It is in your best interest to work out if it's the right fit and say no if it's not.

Not every conversation will end in a sale, and nor should it. When you qualify everybody through this process, you save yourself down the line:

- If you cannot get them closer to the result that they want or need…
- If they are not the right fit for right now…
- If you are not the right expert for them…
  … **do not sell to them!**
- If they are not your dream client…
- If something doesn't feel right…
- If there is a red flag of any sort…
  … **do not sell to them!**

## Conversations: summary

A robust and complete process for conversations with potential clients not only showcases your integrity, but also reduces the risk of misaligned purchasing decisions. The focus is on suitability and service, not getting a sale at all costs. Selling something to someone when it isn't the right fit is not worth it, either for your reputation, your energy or the ultimate result either one of you will get.

| Stage purpose: conversations | To help your hot audience make the right decision for them (no matter the outcome for you). |
|---|---|
| Actions to take in this stage | Take your prospective buyer through your sales conversation process. |

| How you know it's working | You'll make sales. |
|---|---|
| How you know it's not working and what to do about it | You'll be having lots of conversations, but they are not converting to sales. Analyse the data those conversations are giving you: what are they saying and how can you provide more detail on these topics earlier in the process? Are the right people booking onto calls? Tweak and iterate as required. |

## Stage four: Experience and client care

Designing a sales experience that's memorable for all the right reasons is more than worth your while – it feels much nicer to deliver something excellent than something sub-par – but in economic terms, too. Better experiences create more sales! The way you make people feel in the overall experience you provide is your number one brand differentiator and your biggest opportunity. When you focus on the experience as a whole rather than as an individual transaction:

✓ You enable incredible results.
✓ You get more repeat customers.
✓ You can charge higher prices.
✓ You contribute to improving the overall standard in your industry.
✓ People shout you from the rooftops.
✓ Referrals become more likely.

Thinking about your long-term dream client:

- What do you want them to have as a first impression of your business?
- How do you want people to feel about working with you?
- How are you demonstrating this at each stage of the journey?
- Where are you doing things because you think you 'should' rather than because it will actually help your client?
- Are you providing a range of ways for your clients to choose you? No one product will please everyone in your audience. How can you cater to different needs and access points?

The main ways to increase sales are to bring in a steady stream of new customers, for more of those potential clients to buy from you, for those people to buy from you again and again, and then for them to be so delighted with what they bought that they shout about you to all their friends. Having a high-quality client experience impacts three-quarters of those strategies!

Your service has a huge impact on your reputation, which over time can significantly affect your growth. If you become known as someone with a good-quality service, word will spread via word-of-mouth marketing. If you deliver a suboptimal experience, word will spread ten times faster. This can have lasting negative effects, such as:

- The time you spend on social media doesn't create as much traction because people don't want to share your content with their audiences.
- Sales are few and far between and are limited to new customers.
- It is difficult to stand out above the sea of 'same' which impacts you both short and long term.

As purchasers, we want to be well looked after and we are willing to pay significantly more for a luxury product or service. Ensuring the quality of your service is front and centre will pay dividends long term.

So, how can we elevate things so that your client buys something from you and afterwards is left with a lasting impression of how amazing the experience was? How are you making sure your people know that they are in safe hands when they are with you? How are you communicating ahead of time that you are committed to delivering excellence?

Draw from your own personal experience with buying from people. After all, we are all buyers too! The experience you provide is your chance to make your client feel exceptional. Roll out the red carpet: keeping what your client wants at the heart, how can you make this a *dream* for them? Why make someone feel 'just OK' when you can make them feel amazing *and* know that it will serve your business well to go the extra mile?

Use the following prompts to help:

- What is the overall style of your approach? Are you communicating it?
- Pick one word that describes the overarching way you want people to feel in this process of buying from you. What do you want them to feel above all else about buying from you?
- Does every stage of the journey reflect the style and intention you chose above?
- What (if anything) are you doing because you think you 'should' rather than because you want to?
- Do you feel confident about the decision experience you have created?
- Are you supporting your clients through each stage?
- How can you make it even easier for your audience to reach a buying decision?

## Experience: summary

Customer experience elongates client lifetime, promotes loyalty and increases referrals to your business. It's far easier to sell to existing customers who are already familiar with your business and have a relationship with you, than to bring on new ones. When you are able to keep more clients warm to your offers, you don't have to prospect, qualify, or build a relationship all over again for every sale because your business already has built up trust and credibility. Therefore, as well as making you more money, the quality of your experience will also save you time.

| | |
|---|---|
| Stage purpose: experience | To increase client retention, elongate the client relationship and encourage word-of-mouth referrals. |
| Actions to take in this stage | Design an experience that delivers excellence and demonstrate your integrity at every stage. |
| How you know it's working | Clients will leave glowing feedback, want to stay in your world and recommend your business to their friends. |
| How you know it's not working and what to do about it | You won't get repeat business, feedback will be suboptimal or perhaps clients will be dissatisfied. This suggests there's something missing from your current experience: identify this ASAP and decide the right course of action from there. |

**VIP** Have a plan – and stick to it! Sales are the outcome of a simple set of actions (your sales strategy) that you take repeatedly. Knowing what they are allows promoting your products on social media to be fast and effective.

## Lucie Sheridan ... on creating her sales plan and sticking to it

Lucie Sheridan is an artist, illustrator and single mum who designed a one of a kind 'live photo booth' portrait drawing experience. In it, she draws portraits at events in three minutes or less. When I met Lucie she was working part time in the NHS and hoping to transition to full-time self-employment. To do that she needed at least 15 bookings. She asked me to support her to build her sales plan, so that she could realize this goal and feel more stable about taking the business full time. Here's what happened.

*The brief*: secure 15 wedding bookings for her portrait booth, Rubbish Portraits.

*The action broken down into steps*:

**Relevance:**
- Honed in on building awareness within the wedding industry, appealing to couples who wanted unique, personality filled weddings that were more centred around creativity than traditional elements.
- Increased visibility via wedding directories and fairs. Contacted two of the biggest wedding blogs for creative brides and grooms – 'Love My Dress' and the 'Un-Wedding' – and placed features in both.
- Exhibited at the 'Chosen' wedding fair and in the 'Book of Love' directory to be more visible to ideal clients.

*Outcome*: more ideal clients became aware of Rubbish Portraits and how the booth could add something unique to their wedding reception.

**Audience:**
- Used email and regular strategic content on Instagram to nurture and warm up her audience.
- Provided more clear and focused messaging to help new visitors move easily through her buyer journey.
- Created some key content to showcase the desires of her clients, who this was right for and how unique her offering was.
- Tweaked Instagram bio to immediately highlight what people would get from her experience.
- Helped people progress from being a cold audience to actively enquiring by increasing conversation opportunities via following up with interested parties.

*Outcome*: the number of enquiries grew swiftly and steadily.

**Conversations:**
- Confidently leading calls in a more service-led way.
- Following a process rather than 'seeing what happened'.
- Asking structured questions and leading the conversation to assess suitability.
- Taking time to hear about the couple's plans and being clear about whether the product was the right fit.

*Outcome*: conversations converted into bookings more frequently and easily.

**Experience:**
- Being visible and clear about the value in the product at all stages of the process.
- Putting together proposals tailored to and summarizing individual client requirements.
- Encouraging more recommendations and word-of-mouth referrals through quality of experience.

- Elevating the sales experience to showcase awareness of her brand, how much she loves personal connection and creating a fun and unique memory to last.

*Outcome*: more referrals, more raving 'fans' of Rubbish Portraits, more opportunities including being commissioned to draw headshots for, and being championed by, Holly Tucker and the team at Holly and Co.

(Holly Tucker is one of the biggest champions of small business owners in the UK. She is the founder of Holly & Co, a small business advice and inspiration platform which you can delve into here: www.holly.co/)

By putting this structure around her intention Lucie was able to grow her business, create financial stability for her and her daughter and double her target in just a few months. Lucie is now full time in the business, booked out with plentiful clients she loves to draw, and is happily researching the next tax bracket.

You can see Lucie's portrait booth in action on Instagram @lucie_sheridan_live_artist and her amazing illustrations @luciesheridan. I highly recommend both! You can also find Lucie at her website www.luciesheridan.co.uk.

# Now it's your turn!

## To build your step by step sales plan – and stick to it!

Build your sales plan with the help of the four stages and case study above. You are aiming for a list of five to ten key tasks that you will use to achieve relevance, audience nurturing, conversations and deliver high-quality sales experiences.

Download the free resource that accompanies this section for further help, along with all other supporting resources for this book at my website www.saradalrymple.co.uk/moresalesplease.

## Chapter recap

- Strategy is the set of pre-defined actions that keeps your business in funds. There are four stages and they work together. Sales are the outcome of simple, repeatable actions you take to provide a clear and easy experience for your potential clients.
- Use visibility to identify the problems you help your clients fix or improve. Use content to warm your audience up and build connection to you as a personal brand.
- A cold audience isn't ready to buy, they need you to build product awareness first. A warm audience understands the options available and why they're relevant. A hot audience is clear about the overall experience they can expect when buying from you, which brings conviction to their ability to decide what's right for them.

Can you believe we've finished Part II already? Chapters 5, 6 and 7 have been about giving you the confidence to do business your way, and to create experiences that not only elevate the standard for your clients, but that they'll love, too! Never again will you need to flounder over what to do to break down how a sale is made – you now know what to do, the order to do it in and how to align everything to your personality. Refer back to this part every time you need a refresher on how to position something new with clarity.

Now that you have your roadmap, your confidence and your clarity, let's skip on into creating some ease, shall we?

# Part III

# More sales ease

Y ou're ready to start advocating for the work you love to do and to connect with potential clients online. Showing up on social media and being visible in an intentional way, is one way to reach your buyers – fast – and to get their attention through the content you create.

Being a small business owner in the digital age presents an enormous opportunity, and everything in this part exists to help you take full advantage of that by making it as easy as possible for you to promote with consistency. Only four out of ten business owners are harnessing the power of social media effectively:[1] I want to see more people using it and making sales from doing so.

I don't believe that slogging it out for hours on social media is a good use of your time, so I'm showing you how to structure your content to build traction and advocate for sales in whatever time you have available. When you combine your step-by-step sales plan created in this chapter with the magic of social media, you get to do this in minutes instead of hours. Bingo!

You will discover:

- how to use your own experiences and stories to fuel your business;
- how to create content with ease: your 30 days of implementation;
- the magic of social media in connecting you to dream clients in just minutes each day.

This final part shows you how to become the voice of your business, finding your ease with showing up and using the content you create to attract a steady stream of new clients. When visibility and self-promotion become effortless and automatic, you attract new clients the sustainable way, increasing sales and growing your impact.

---

[1] www.independent.co.uk/news/business/uk-businesses-social-media-poll-b1852747.html

# Chapter 8

# Harnessing the power of your personal brand

*Everyone has a personal brand. The difference is whether or not you choose to maximize it.*

(Lucy Werner, PR expert and hype maestro)

I wrote the first 20,000 words of this book in Dubai. I wanted to focus on writing in my happy place: the sunshine, away from my daily responsibilities, away from February in England and the wet, grey scene that is London in winter, away from all of it. So, after not very much persuading at all, I roped my friend Katie into coming with me, took five days off, packed my laptop and my notes, and boarded the plane.

Committed to hitting my daily goal, I would get up early, crank out a couple of hours before breakfast, hit up the breakfast buffet (hard – I can't say no!), sit al fresco with my laptop, sip on delicious coffee that I hadn't had to make, and generally press right on until such time as I hit 4,000 words. At which point I would punch the air, douse myself in suncream and scuttle to the nearest sun lounger to join Katie for a couple of hours of glorious chillaxing. There we'd stay, before going for dinner, getting an early night, and starting all over again the next day. It worked like a charm. There's not much I won't do for a couple of hours in the sun, and if that meant being focused so I could hit my word count, so be it.

On our last day, we visited the Atlantis The Royal hotel, which had opened two weeks prior. In the cab, Katie casually told me Beyoncé had performed there on opening night for a cool US$24 million fee.

## Beyoncé × small business

Beyoncé is absolutely at the top of her game. She is determined, she has been working for decades. She's been showing up and giving mind-blowing experiences to people who go to her shows since her Destiny's Child days, and right now, her Renaissance world tour is generating billions of dollars in income globally. What point am I making here? That's easy: I'm telling you to stop playing small and be more Beyoncé.

Imagine if young Beyoncé with all that talent, her epic voice, her power and her moves, had never gone for it in the way that she has. Imagine if she kept all those moves confined to dance routines learned with friends in the school playground, or her voice confined to singing in her bedroom.

I'm not saying you need to become a pop superstar, but imagine the additional impact you could have if you were more visible and more people knew you existed. If you weren't hiding your skills from 99.9% of the World Wide Web.

I'm always wanging on about the huge impact the small business community could have on the economy if they felt more comfortable showing up and being seen. We could literally boost it by millions – or even billions – if more business owners found it easier to show up and get visible. Your product can be world class, but it doesn't count for a thing if you don't also go out there and connect with the people who will buy it. Having an amazing singing voice like Beyoncé is only half the job. Just like being in a blockbuster movie is only half the job for Arnie.

What that means for your small business is that creating your product is only half the job: it's not enough on its own to create consistent sales. Your product can be the best in the world and still your business will completely fail if you keep it a secret and nobody knows about it. You also need to advocate for why people should buy your products.

So I say we all start playing a bit bigger than 'just enough to get by'. I say we all start taking a leaf out of Ms Beyoncé Knowles' books and don't stop until we get wherever it is we want to go. After all, she's single handedly responsible for spiking inflation in Sweden and pretty much every other place her tour has been this year.[2]

Let's start with a small but mighty game changer: you finding your feet with getting visible by using the biggest USP you have: *yourself*, aka your personal brand.

## What is a personal brand?

Your personal brand is how to create the connection with your audience that drives demand for what you're selling.

People buy from people. Yes, they absolutely need you to talk about what you're selling and explain to them who your products are for, but initially they just want to know and connect with you. As we saw in Chapter 5, Gerald Zaltman said so. Connection comes from sharing more than just what you sell. Your audience wants to know who you are outside of the business, and when they feel they do, they appreciate the honesty and the fact that you've shared your experiences with them. Knowing personal things about people accelerates connection and makes us more likely to stick around.

Connection creates demand for your products. When you use your platform to share stories and create a narrative around what you're doing – well – that builds the connection that changes everything. This is why the vast majority of people in your audience won't buy on the first day they find you: they don't have a connection with your business yet, so they don't

2 www.theguardian.com/music/2023/jun/15/beyonce-concert-in-stockholm-blamed-for-unexpectedly-high-swedish-inflation

care enough to make a purchase yet. Over time, your content will allow that connection to grow and be nurtured – awareness of your brand builds and people get to know more about the products you sell – and why. Eventually, that connection will become strong enough that a buying decision is forthcoming.

Your personal brand is the action you take to inform the way other people perceive you. It is the platform you build for your own voice to be heard: your message, the things you represent and the change you want to make in the world. This gives your business additional opportunities to connect with a wider audience, and is one of the main reasons to get visible and share your values and stories online.

Your personal brand is how you establish a meaningful connection with your new audience and people who don't know you yet. It's the story you tell that makes everything you do make sense. It builds demand for what you sell by giving context. Stories help us find and build human connection and common ground, and putting the human side to our business out online accelerates that connection. This is the power of your personal brand: it shortens the amount of time it can take for clients to move through the decision-making pathway. Ergo, your personal brand is a powerful sales tool and if you're only using the internet to talk about your products without putting them into context, you're missing a *huge* piece of the pie.

Selling isn't only about products, it's about relationships, experiences and meaningful moments, too. Real connections. Trust. Shared experience. Therefore, being visible and building your personal brand creates interest and a greater degree of authenticity to your business and all that you sell. Products sell so much better when there is genuine attraction to what you do and how you do it. As a small business owner, your story is your superpower. It gives your product relevance, context, direct applications and allows your audience to see what you do in the exact way you want it to be seen.

Making connections that lead to sales is not just about sharing what you do, it's also about sharing things about *you* that make you unique. The things that make you 'you', from the values you hold to the experiences you've had to date, to your personality. This is your personal brand and when it comes to showing up online, plays a significant role in the success you'll have with making sales.

Your personal brand tells the story of who you are outside the products you sell, that helps your audience connect not just with your business, but also with you as a person. It helps people who don't know you yet, buy into the reason behind what you do. It brings everything that you're about together in a way that makes sense – both to you and to your audience – to make it relevant for why your business exists.

A strong personal brand is the thing that brings you more opportunities to get paid to do what you love. When you have a strong personal brand, you are connecting with people not just because your skillset matches their current needs, but on a human-to-human level. This opens up your appeal beyond what you're selling right now, protects you from comparison and strengthens the connection between you and your audience.

Your personal brand helps you know what to post, how to present yourself online today, and for where you're going next. Other people's perception of you is a direct response to how you talk about yourself. Therefore, by taking control of this narrative you can make it easier for people to see you in the way that you want to be seen.

When you think about it, paying attention to your personal brand also future proofs your business. It allows you to pivot in a new direction if you desire, to bring out a new range of products just because you felt like it, or to run multiple businesses side by side because once the wider context exists, it opens up the floodgates for so many different directions.

---

**How your personal brand benefits your business:**

✓ Builds deeper and faster connection.

✓ Opens up opportunities outside of current product suite.

✓ Future proofs business.

✓ Helps you sell your products no matter how small your audience is.

✓ Protects from reputational risk.

✓ Adds a more cohesive feel to your brand.

✓ Encourages clients not just to buy from you once, but over and over again.

---

# Personal brand for sales

Really effective personal brand content will build meaningful connection with your target client in a fraction of the time.

## Share your point of view

How do you see the world differently? You don't need a brand new concept or innovative way of working to stand out and capture the attention of your clients. What can really set you apart from others in your area of work is your individual viewpoint and how you apply what you know. Having your own stance on an existing problem or situation helps your audience see your perspective. For example, within your industry or audience there will be issues and problems and situations that are familiar and widely acknowledged. Developing a clear perspective or point of view around why this happens and how to solve them will provide much needed differentiation and help people connect more specifically with you, not just because of what you do.

## The sweet spot

Find the intersection between something your audience can relate to personally *and* something you have the desire to change or improve in the world. Achieve relevance and get attention from your core audience all in one, by finding the point at which your personal interests and your business skills cross. Knowing this point, and creating content around it, will ensure the time you spend being visible creates value for your business.

- What do you want your audience to know about what's driving you personally?
- What's your unique point of view on the subject matter within your industry?
- How do you connect your skillset with the wider world?

A super common mistake I see is assuming these things are obvious. Unless you weave them into your narrative: they're not.

## Share your expertise with the people you want to work with

Taking ownership of your skills, expertise and unique points of view is what makes up the fabric of your visibility efforts. Sharing content that tells stories about all three and allows your audience to get to know you without having to move from the social media platform or website they're on is important from a service perspective. It makes it easy for people to pick up your content at moments that are opportune for them. It meets them where they are. And it allows them to consider how your opinions fit with their own, on certain, key topics.

## Be genuine and authentic

Be 100% yourself. Fly the flag for whatever it is that makes you, you! element of your personal brand. Mix up your content so that you tell people who you are, what you stand for and the journey of how you got to where you are today. In doing so you will capture the imagination of your audience and unearth any points of commonality they may share. And, for goodness sake, please use your own tone of voice. If we are not authentic we won't connect with our clients. The definition of authentic is genuine, real (not false), not copied.[3] When we try to be something we are not people can tell and so can we: it doesn't feel good. That affects body language, eye contact, language, how we behave, how we respond. All of these elements are key factors of selling and must be natural responses.

> Be yourself! People buy from people first. Showcasing your personal brand and the human side of your business helps people feel connected to you, which increases sales.

### Lucy Werner on ... growing her business by being herself, harnessing the power of her personal brand

Lucy Werner is a PR and personal brand expert. She is the author of two books (*Hype Yourself* and *Brand Yourself*) – it's fair to say she knows her stuff when it comes to the power of a strong personal brand. So obviously I had to ask her to share some of her wisdom with us here:

'Harnessing the power of personal brand has been a complete game changer for my business. It's helped me raise my profile, get booked for speaking, teaching and workshops, attract more clients and expand into new areas. I now have ten different revenue streams including books, courses, education and brand partnerships – all of which are flexible while also paying the bills, just how I like it with three young children at home!

Everyone has a personal brand by their digital footprint. The difference is whether or not you choose to maximize it. I try to seize every opportunity and stick to my geek zone – PR and personal brand advice. I think of

---

[3] https://dictionary.cambridge.org/dictionary/english/authentic

creative ways to show my personal brand, from hiding my books in fun places where my target audience will find them, to always having a copy of my book with me. This meant I was able to give one to the legendary Chris Do, becoming a guest on his podcast and now teaching for The Futur. My work is now global, fully remote and I've even relocated to the countryside in the South of France.

Personal brand is about building a connection with your audience outside of the products and services you're selling. The importance of building emotional connection through storytelling is a non-negotiable in my sales process, because I want people to know the person they'll be working with – me!

I share things like my PR take on topical Netflix shows, stories in the news or great examples of other creative entrepreneurs. I also talk about my life relocating to the South of France, co-working with the co-founder of my children and things that inspire me. I like to think of it as like showing a bit of ankle, a pinch of your personality for your audience.'

 **Lucy's top tip**

If you are starting out on your personal brand, be really clear on your values. Pick 3–5 and before you work with any one client, brand partner, podcast host, ask yourself if they align with these. Let them guide you in your decision-making process and to keep you true to who you are.'

Find Lucy on Instagram @lucywernerpr or at her website www.thewern.com. She's a well of knowledge for DIY publicity and profile building which she shares generously with her audience – absolutely one of the biggest champions of small business around.

# Now it's your turn!

## To grow your business by being yourself

What feels important for your audience to know about you? As humans we are all multifaceted and have hundreds of stories we could tell, but from the perspective of helping your clients, which are the most relevant stories? Are you intentionally creating content that supports this narrative?

Think about how you can harness the power of your personal brand to grow your sales.

- Make a list of key things you stand for both in and outside your business. What points of commonality can you spot between you and your ideal client?
- What are the defining points on the journey you've taken to arrive at where you are today? Are there any stories here that overlap with what your audience is looking to achieve now?
- Do you have a unique perspective or opinion to share? Do you see the world differently to others in your industry or niche?
- How much of the above are you sharing with your audience? Can you bring more of it into the conversation?

Create a personal brand mood board where you keep inspiring brand elements, from colours, to fonts, to photography that you are drawn to. I have created a personal brand photography Pinterest board for inspiration. You can find it, along with the other resources that accompany this book at: www.saradalrymple.co.uk/moresalesplease along with all the other accompanying resources for this book.

# Chapter recap

- Sales are built from connection and ease. Visibility creates ease for clients and making your presence easy to find is all part of the service. Personal brand and the content you share creates connection between you and your audience. Connection creates demand for your products. Both are helpful for sales.

- Your clients buy into people first, then your products. Sharing stories, your values and establishing shared experiences all help with this.
- Getting visible and sharing key points in your personal brand are key, especially in the beginning while building brand awareness.
- Your personal brand is how you take control of your own narrative, which in turn allows you to tap into more opportunities both now and in the future. Always be genuine and tell your story – your audience can tell when you're trying to be someone you're not.

This chapter has shown the advantages of being yourself and having a strong sense of your personal brand. From a sales perspective it speeds up connection, builds demand and creates new opportunities. We've used the activity above to start thinking about the narrative you want to put out on social media, which is handy because that's where we're heading next!

# Chapter 9

# Turning content into sales

*Plant a seed every day that helps people buy in the future.*
(Josephine Brooks, sustainable marketing expert)

Missed the class in school where they taught you how to create compelling content for use on the internet? Me too. I'm well into my forties so we barely even *had* the internet when I was at school! Fear not though, I've figured it out now and I've got you covered. When you're first getting into a rhythm with creating sales content it happens easier with a framework to follow. And across the next two chapters, that's exactly what you'll get.

## The magic of social media

Thinking about the additional economic impact small businesses could have, it's hard to think of a better place to do the heavy lifting for you than social media. With less than half of business owners confidently using social media to promote what they do, and the majority who are feeling invisible despite their efforts, there is a huge opportunity to improve.

Social media is a powerful way to market your business and build deeper connections in just a few minutes of focus. The most important step is to get started. The second most important step is to keep going! The content you post on social media will tell your audience everything they need to know, if you let it. The magic of social media is that you can use it to allow your content to reach potentially thousands of people in just a few minutes each day.

This chapter will show you what to focus on when using social media as a business tool to make sure:

- The time you spend on social media is giving you a return, i.e. it actually increases demand for your products and brings you sales.
- You are clear about how social media fits into your overall sales plan. For example, will you use it purely as a visibility tool to attract clients, or to support all stages of the sales process?
- The content you're creating for social media has a specific purpose, i.e. you are not creating content at random. It is crucial that you create content in line with the stage(s) of the sales process you're using social media to support.

There are three things your audience needs from you before they will buy, and social media is an easy way to deliver all three:

1. Connection with you as a person.
2. Confidence in you as an authority: are you going to get them the result they crave?
3. Conviction in their decision making.

To solve this they need:

- A message that's clear: what's in it for them?
- A way for them to hear this multiple times. (Most people don't buy the first time they hear about something. In fact, the Marketing Rule of 7 suggests that a potential buyer needs to see something seven times before buying it.)[1]
- Human connection and service.

---

[1] https://startups.co.uk/guides/rule-of-seven/

- Confidence in their ability to get the result you're promising.
- To be invited in regularly.

The conduit for all of these is your content. By creating the types of content that actually help your audience buy from you, and putting it on social media, you unlock its true magic: consistent sales with ease.

## Selling on social media

Social media gives us a place to show up, connect with clients and advocate for what you're all about in business. It's a brilliant (and free!) place to increase that all important visibility and to get in front of ideal buyers – many of whom use social media straight from the phones in their hand, multiple times a day. No amount of in-person networking will get you in front of as many ideal clients as quickly as social media can.

Use the time you spend on social media strategically. You are there to create sales for your small business, build brand awareness and connect with potential clients. The goal is not to be an 'influencer' which (although still awesome) carries a completely different set of desired outcomes and strategies to get there.

For small business owners looking to create consistent sales, the key is to use social media to take small repeatable actions, aka your sales activity, have it take minutes each day, and get on with the rest of your day, safe in the knowledge that you're keeping your audience regularly furnished with relevant information that helps them make easier decisions. When you do this, you'll have an established network of previous buyers, who are either buying from you again and again (yay!), telling their friends about you (yay!), leaving reviews (yay!) or putting your name forward for speaking opportunities (yay!).

# Why spend time selling on social media?

It's simple really – your ideal client is on there:

- 84.3% of the UK population uses social media platforms.
- As of January 2022, there were 57.60 million social media users in the UK.
- There were 32.3 million Instagram users in the UK in September 2022.
- 73% of people in the UK use Facebook or Instagram daily.[2]

This is a *big opportunity* for small business owners: it's how to increase awareness for your business, improve the customer experience, shorten the amount of time it takes for people to buy, and create opportunities for sales. Data from Meta, the parent company of Instagram, Facebook and WhatsApp, show that 83% of Instagram users say they have discovered new brands while on the platform.[3]

Selling on social media presents all business owners with a unique opportunity: to really serve the heck out of every single buyer in a way that suits individual personalities. This is especially true for small business owners, who now have a way to bring human connection and personality to scale and to stay front of mind.

By combining service, human connection and speaking to a need, selling on social media is almost all positioning and hardly any actual 'selling'. When the information is laid out in such a well thought-out way, people can walk as far along the journey as they feel comfortable to, and opt in to buying from you almost entirely by themselves. Not all of them will want to, not all of you will want them to, and of course we're on hand for all the chats required where necessary, but equally, if somebody

---

[2] https://moneyzine.com/uk/resources/social-media-statistics-uk/
[3] https://startupbonsai.com/instagram-marketing-statistics/

is ready to buy now – the option is there for them to do so where appropriate for your business model.

When people buy from small business owners, they are not choosing you because of price – they are choosing you because they like what they've seen of your business. It could be that they align with your values, the way you operate or because they have something in common with you. When you prioritize showing up with a clear proposition for the people who need it, and blending this in with connecting on a human level, sales will happen without you having to chase them down.

## How to use social media

When used with intention, social media is a powerful relationship-building and sales machine that can singlehandedly connect you to thousands of ideal clients, nurture your audience and create lots of sales, all from your phone or computer in a few minutes each day. There are more than 4.59 billion active users of social media today, and this number is expected to increase to almost 6 billion by 2027.[4]

Make no mistake – social media has the power to totally transform the results you get in your business and save you countless hours in the process. Use the methodology in the next two chapters to create momentum for your business and to:

- get in front of thousands of ideal clients;
- establish genuine connection through your personal brand;
- nurture your audience;
- create demand for your products;
- have conversations with interested parties;
- make sales.

---

[4] www.statista.com/statistics/260811/social-network-penetration-worldwide

# Using social media to support every stage of the sales process

Social media is a fantastically flexible way to promote what you do and amplify your visibility. You can use it to support all parts of the sales process, or just to raise awareness about what you do. You get to choose how much or how little social media supports your business.

Being a small business owner doesn't require you to master all platforms or become an influencer to be able to use social media to skyrocket your sales. Choose a platform that is well suited to your personality and use it strategically for the parts of the sales process you'd like it to support you with.

---

**Ways social media can help your business**

✓ Use social media to drive traffic to your website (for example by having a link in your LinkedIn/Facebook/Instagram bio).

✓ Give potential buyers a taste of what your business is about by sharing visual elements to your feed.

✓ Create intrigue and give insight into the product creation process, by sharing behind the scenes videos or photos of how you select the materials you work with, your workspace set up or the thing you're working on right now.

✓ Deepen connection with your audience in real time, by sharing stories on relevant topics.

✓ Start conversations through the content you create. Instagram, Facebook, LinkedIn and X all have multiple ways to create interactive content that promotes conversations with the people consuming it.

---

✓  Conduct market research and gain real-time insights into the needs of your audience. Poll the people who follow you on their views on a certain topic, invite them to choose the product you create next by selecting from a shortlist, ask them for their perspectives – bring them into the conversation.

✓  Showcase your personal brand and stand out from the rest of your industry. Create content that is unmistakably you – share your opinions, have a strong sense of self and make sure your unique lens is put on everything you share with your audience so that they can see you in a crowd.

# Choosing the right social media platform for you

Whether you're just getting started or looking to expand your existing presence, with so much choice available it can be tempting to be 'everywhere'. The danger is trying to learn how to leverage multiple platforms can become overwhelming and lead to not getting results. In general, I recommend picking one platform to begin with and focusing on mastering how to use it as well as you can. Then, when that's up and running and performing well in terms of your specific goals, you can add more platforms in later on.

The current main platforms are:

- **Facebook:** The most used platform. Allows you to create a bespoke page for your business, as well as groups within which you can grow bespoke audiences of potential clients or other business owners. You can also post photos and Stories, direct from Instagram.
- **Instagram:** With the ability to share video content, photos and written pieces across a variety of content

types, consider promoting your business on Instagram if sharing a combination of different content types appeals to you/your audience, who can then share and save it to refer back to with ease.

- **TikTok:** Video sharing app which has rapidly become one of the most widely use platforms, especially among younger audiences.
- **X:** X is a text only platform where you can post shortform messages, or 'tweets'. These tweets are a great way to get a short bit of information out to followers, whether it's an announcement about a product, a link to a blog post, or a poll you're using to gather information. It's a great place to create a consistent voice that aligns with your values, all in a 280-character limit.
- **LinkedIn:** LinkedIn is the world's largest professional network and provides myriad ways to share opinion pieces, links to blog posts, reviews and work experience.
- **Pinterest:** A visual driven search engine that serves as a place for inspiration and productivity.
- **YouTube:** an online video sharing and social media platform perfect for educating your audience on your core topics by providing useful trainings.

## Understand the different platforms and their uses

Each platform has its own personality and style. For example, X is fast-paced and focuses on trending topics. LinkedIn allows you to share expertise and company information. Instagram and TikTok have a lot of video and photo functionality built in, while Facebook allows you to create Groups.

## Where is your audience most likely to be?

Your potential buyers are absolutely the number one factor for consideration when choosing your social media platform: Go where they are. Age, demographics and consumer behaviour all play a part here. If your audience isn't active on the channel you spend the most time on, you won't get the traction you're looking for. For example, Facebook might be one of the platforms you are more familiar with due to it being one of the first, but if all your clients are hanging out on TikTok that's where you need to be, too.

## Which is the best fit for your business?

Consider what you're selling – if you have physical products to sell, a more visual platform may suit you better than a more text-based app. Likewise, if you're someone who finds it easier to create video content than written, consider this in your selection, too.

## How will the channel help you reach your goal?

What are you looking to get out of spending time on social media? Is it networking opportunities? Building awareness for your products? Explaining them to new audiences?

How many leads are you hoping for? How many sales do you want? What are you getting visible to achieve? Use social media as a positioning tool to aid that goal.

If you need a platform that allows you to share content in a certain way, make sure you're choosing the best fit. Not all platforms are going to make sense for your business, so remember to focus on meeting your customers and prospects where they are.

# Creating content for sales

Content for social media as a business owner is all about ensuring:

1. the time you spend on visibility activity actually builds traction for your business;
2. it's easy for you to create the right type of content every time.

There are actually only a few types of content you need to create regularly for steady sales on the internet. When you know the type of content that converts... you attract ideal clients and consistently convert into sales, you make more money, and your content takes you less time.

When you know the content people want to see, the type that speaks to your ideal client and moves them through your buyer experience, it speeds up the amount of time it takes for sales to be made. You no longer spend hour upon hour creating content that gets your audience precisely nowhere. When you know what to say you can hit a rhythm faster and you get more people coming to you, engaging with you, wanting to buy from you.

I think this is the right time to give you a quick reminder. *Your content is not supposed to appeal to every living soul on the internet.* It has the specific purpose of calling in people with both of these things: the specific need you can solve *and* the finances and motivation to make a change.

There are a *lot* of people who will have one or the other of these things but not both. These people are not your clients, and therefore shouldn't be anywhere near your consciousness when you're creating content.

People your content is *not* for:

- Your colleagues or industry peers.
- People you went to school with who randomly follow you online.
- Friends and family.

People your content *is* for:

- People who are actively looking for the thing you're selling. These could be people who are already in your audience, or people who are not yet aware of you. If the former, your content needs to move them through the journey. If the latter, your content needs to do the job of getting their attention. Either way, your content has a job to do.

OK now we've got that clear, here are the only three content types you need for sales.

# The three types of content that turn followers into buyers

Knowing the type of content people want to see and using that knowledge to share content that speaks to your ideal client means you can create content efficiently and to maximum benefit. Ultimately, this means taking people through the decision-making process as quickly as they want to go. Posting photos of fancy breakfasts and walks in the park are cute, but they don't help people progress through the decision-making journey about whether to buy from you.

The following foundational content pieces not only attract dream clients but also allow you to translate the time you spend online being visible, into sales. Having awareness of these content types stops you wasting time showing up with filler content that isn't the right kind to convert followers to buyers.

| Filler content | Sales content |
|---|---|
| Cute meals you've eaten or places you've visited that have nothing to do with your client | Content that builds meaningful connection |
| Wishy washy or vague mentions of your products with no context | Content that builds confidence in you |
| Inspirational quotes you saw on the internet | Content that builds conviction in decision making |

## Connection content

Connection content is how you greet new people into your world. It helps the colder end of your audience who don't know you yet, find those initial threads of curiosity that will capture their imagination and make them want to find out more. Connection content incorporates stories and personal brand elements that draw people into your world, as well as giving evidence of the type of information you share on your topic.

## Confidence content

Confidence content warms your audience up further by nurturing them and deepening connection. Confidence content shares what you're thinking and doing, together with lessons, experiences, things you've learned and your beliefs. It's also an opportunity to combine your views and share bite-sized teaching moments or education around your topic.

## Conviction content

This is the type of content that allows your audience to get to know their options *and* activates them to make a decision. Without this type of content in your strategy, you'll create a legion of loyal followers who don't necessarily convert to sales (because you didn't ask them to). The goal with conviction content is to allow people to feel sure in their decision making.

You'll find lots of examples of each of the three content types in the 30-day challenge in Chapter 10.

> Marry up your content to reflect whichever stage of the sales process you're using social media to support you with.

### Josephine Brooks on ... using social media in a way that suits you

Josephine Brooks is a marketing expert with a passion for building business in a sustainable way and not burning out. I asked her about her experiences growing her brand on and off social media and I love how easy it is to see from her story that you can use social media for as little or as much of your overall sales process as you wish. There is no one right or wrong way when it comes to promoting your business - the key is to find what works best for you.

'Social media is an amazing place to connect with people from all over the world, but doesn't have to be the place where your whole marketing strategy takes place if you don't want it to.

It's important to me that my marketing plan is sustainable. Marketing, selling and delivering excellent results for my clients are my most important tasks and, over time, I've refined how I do this in the right way for me. As an introvert I prefer blending evergreen marketing with social media and having the two work together so that social media isn't something I'm solely relying on to drive sales. I generally use social media as a nurture platform and a place to signpost my followers to my email list, blog posts and my podcast.

With evergreen/sustainable marketing (YouTube videos, blog posts, podcasts) you're planting a seed every day that helps people buy in the future. For me, social media is fun when it's the cherry on the cake (not the whole cake).

Small repeatable actions that help me include keeping to routine with my marketing. This will be different for everyone, but for me right now it looks like a blog post a week, an email each week, a podcast episode every week, then 2–3 social media posts. I start with the blog post, then I'll repurpose it into email and Instagram posts, then finally I record the podcast episode. Building that habit has really helped me stay consistent.'

**Josephine's top tip**

Set a routine for how you're going to use the platforms you most align with. It's much better to do key, repeatable things well than to spread yourself too thin. Then stick to it! So, for example, you might use email and send email once a week and use social media three times a week. Make that the first thing you do each day. Spend more time repeating the same core messages over and over again. Your client needs to hear the same thing multiple times before they will decide to buy – you don't always have to reinvent the wheel or start from scratch. Less is more!

Find Josephine on Instagram @josephinepbrooks or head on over to her website www.josephinebrooks.co.uk where she has an array of fantastically useful blog posts on this topic.

# Now it's your turn!

## To decide the role social media will play in your sales strategy

- Look back at Chapter 7 and the sales plan you made. How do you want to use social media to support you with this? Do you want to use it to help you purely with the initial 'relevance' phase and to get you in front of more ideal clients, or will you use it to support every stage of the sales process? Being clear on how you're going to use it will help you stay clear on the types of content to focus on.
- If you are using social media to support all phases in your sales plan, be sure to balance the content you create across all three types (connection, confidence

and conviction content). We will explore this in detail in Chapter 10.

• Next, pick a primary social media platform. Which one feels most aligned for you and your ideal client? The sweet spot is one that suits your personality, while also being where your audience hangs out.

## Chapter recap

• Social media is a powerful sales-generating machine, but it doesn't have to be where all your marketing and sales activity takes place if you don't want it to be. You can use it for as little or as much of your sales process as you like.

• There are three types of content to create that will help people at all stages of the journey. These are: confidence content, connection content and conviction content.

• Choose your platform based on the goals of your business, where your audience hangs out, and your preferences.

• Always create content for the stage of the sales process you're using social media to support you with. For example, if you're prioritizing being seen by new clients, make sure your activity includes lots of collaborations where you're getting in front of the right people. If you're using it to warm up existing audience members, make sure your content gives them clear, confidence-boosting messages. This avoids 'filler' content that isn't relevant for your goal.

Now you know how you'll use social media to support your sales plan, and the types of content that will help your audience progress to a decision, all that remains is to put one foot in front of the other and start! Let's canter into Chapter 10 for your 30-day action plan!

# Chapter 10
# Self-promotion made simple

*No matter what you think, you are not selling too much!*
(Tamu Thomas, emotional well-being coach)

In 1990, when I was around nine or ten years old, Saturday mornings were unwaveringly made up of two key activities: swimming lessons and buying stickers. The swimming lessons were OK, and sure, adding to the badge collection my mum would then sew on my towel was cool, but the stickers – oh the stickers! Those were obsession level ten and the thing I waited for all week.

Let me explain something to you in case you're younger than me and wondering what on earth I'm on about. In the late eighties and early nineties, we didn't have the internet, mobile phones or even more than about three channels on TV. Unlikely as it may now sound, stickers were a *very big deal* in playgrounds up and down the country.

Furries, shinies, and everything in between would be eagerly traded come Monday morning break. Rain or shine, the market was fast and fierce and there was a constant need for new supply. What a time to be alive!

In my little hometown, that meant the best place (the only place) to head to after swimming, was straight to a lovely little gift shop that was called At Present. In I'd go, straight from the pool, hair wet and global hypercolour t-shirt always on, where I'd scurry straight to the back where the sticker stash was. There, I'd eyeball the rolls of stickers and spend as many pennies as my mum would allow on the latest furry friends and shiny rainbows.

There was quite an art to this: the trick wasn't to only buy what you wanted to keep – oh no – it was to take a punt on what would be the rarest and most sought-after sticker in the playground. You see this little shop was in a different town to lots of my friends, and their local shops would all have different stickers. And so, come Monday, the trading would commence and the payoffs were only as good as the fresh stock you had in your hand. The thrill of going into that little shop was constant. It never disappointed. And minutes later, out I'd go, with a spring in my step that took me all the way to Tuesday.

The lady who worked in the shop would have something new and exciting in her sticker stash, and she knew exactly how sought after that was to the junior school kids of the time. So, when we came in, do you know what she *didn't* do? She didn't look apologetic and say, 'I've got some new stickers, I'm sorry'. Of course she didn't! She said, 'Come this way and have a look at the brilliant new arrivals that have come in this week'.

Next time you're tempted to bring an air of apology to your promoting, remember how strange that is. Why are you apologizing for delivering on someone's favourite pastime? Isn't it more fun to create a rompingly excellent experience that gets everyone excited, instead?

## Wherever you are on the journey, just start

What I know to be true is that absolutely anyone can learn how to sell well. But that's not to say we all start out feeling like natural born salespeople automatically on our first day in business. Depending on your starting point, promoting yourself and learning to love the way you sell things is a journey.

For some people it can genuinely be as carefree from the start as running barefoot through a flower meadow on a balmy summer's day. For the majority, it feels more like a voyage through the choppy waters of self-discovery, past the perils of permission and eventually, something that becomes a natural part of running a business. No point beating around the bush – most people need some time to go from never having 'put themselves out there' to showing up comfortably.

In much the same way that reading a book on how to run a marathon doesn't mean you can run those 26 miles in your target time the very next day, mastering the art of self-promotion requires taking action, too. So before we can go any further and get into motion, we need to tackle the giant elephant in the room.

## Why on earth is self-promotion so awkward?

Yep, there's an elephant alright. Let's call it 'the gargantuan fear of being judged'. This familiar but cruel mistress has likely been walking in close proximity to you for yonks, if not your entire life in one way shape or form.

Does this ever happen to you? You wake up in the morning and spring out of bed like the empowered business owner you are, ready to 'slay the day' and 'make it happen'. As you drink your morning coffee you marvel at the opportunity that each new day presents in the life of #beingyourownboss and luxuriate in the flexible freedom it affords you. After all, you can do anything!

Then, all of a sudden, it's time to do something in particular – your promotional activity – and just like that, your whole demeanour transforms. Just the thought of talking to strangers on the internet and – gasp! – people seeing you sharing your opinions has you overcome with sweaty palms, next level self-critique and a chronic phobia of looking pushy or being 'too much'. It doesn't take long for you to become so consumed with *not* looking like a total douche in front of the whole World Wide Web that not only do you peg it through your points, but you also forget the whole reason to be visible. Which is actually not about you at all, it is to serve your audience and to furnish them with the confidence they need to make decisions. You are so distracted by what you imagine strangers on the internet, Auntie Doris or someone you haven't clapped eyes on since your minor flirtation at the school leavers disco in 1998 think, that what ensues can at best be described as a rushed, highly cringeworthy and substandard attempt at Styling. It. Out. No wonder these endeavours, the direct conversations you have with clients and the sales that ensue are so few and far between!

Yep, this is fear of judgement in action, as sure as eggs are eggs. As well as being a huge, miserable barrier to your hopes and dreams, her real danger is that she has been running the show for so long she feels comfy and like common sense. Your protector, your safe zone. She has casually got you thinking she's how to navigate the world unscathed. Don't put yourself out there – stay here with me. Safety by stealth: stay small and under the radar. Raise your head above the parapet – are you mad? Who knows what happens when you do *that*? Well me, I do. And I'm going to tell you.

The first time you do it, it feels awkward and unrewarding. Much like the first time you try to ride a bike or put your hand up to say something in class: a lot of potential risk for minimal reward.

The second time you do it, it's less of a big deal. Before you know it, you're getting into your groove, and somewhere along the line you realize you've got the hang of it. It's not even a thing you have to think about anymore, you just do it, the same way you brush your teeth in the morning. And then, you find clients who are excited to see you, you talk to them, and then you get paid to deliver the exact work you love to do. Bingo!

No scary stories to report whatsoever. As yet, I haven't been carted off to see the mayor of social media to be struck off for sharing about *my business* on *my social media* page with *my audience*. I've checked the terra, and its firma. Thou art safe to proceed.

Deep down, you know you're not going to let a cruddy piece of conditioning that pre-dates even that aforementioned awkward disco encounter from 1998 hold you back from making a ruddy good go of this business. You wouldn't be reading this book if you were. So with that, I come bearing the gift of freedom from the shackles keeping you small: it's safe to stop lambasting yourself with the horrors of what people *could* say about you according to the depths of your wildest imagination. It's not what happens when you share useful information about your products, it's just not.

Here are my recommendations for how you can go forth into action taking and self-promote without feeling like the biggest chump on the planet.

## Be yourself

The best way I've found to get your promotion mojo (promojo?) on is just to be yourself, right where you are. You're not trying to transform yourself into someone you're not, so this isn't about getting overexuberant with the jazz hands or morphing into an overexcited extrovert if your natural state is cool, calm and 100% collected. Ditch the myths, remember? Visibility is about creating ease for your clients, and opportunities for connection to grow. That's all. Before they will buy, people need to trust you, and the easiest way to create trust is to be genuine. If you're trying to sound a certain type of way, something is going to feel off to your client, and this interferes with their ability to trust you.

For the avoidance of any doubt, the *only* way to be when you're showing up online or trying to sell something (or writing this book!) is the same way you would talk to your friends when you meet them for lunch or at the pub. Jargon is out, clarity is in. Be colloquial, be informal, be *yourself*.

## Stop assuming nobody wants to hear about your products

Why do people do this?

Marilyn Monroe said, 'Happiness is not in money, but in shopping'. And last time I checked there were millions of people out there who would absolutely agree.

Think about it. Do you recoil in horror when your favourite fashion label sends word of a 50% off sale? Is there a world in which you'd be in any way irritated by getting first dibs on tickets to Glastonbury 24 hours before tickets go on sale to the general public? Would you be livid if Wimbledon popped into your inbox to offer you front row seats at the final?

Surely, if these are things you actually *want*, you're likely to be *thrilled* that someone gently let you know your window of opportunity, no? When you want things, it's nice to be reminded when they go on sale or how to get your hands on them. In fact, it's more than nice, who likes nice? It's positively excellent!

Your marketing spaces are your virtual 'shop window'. People that have signed up to receive your emails, are following you on social media or are browsing your blog *want* to hear from you. Stop assuming they don't or apologizing for talking about the products and services that actually help them! We need reminders, they're helpful! We are also busy. We forget things. We appreciate the nudge. Multiple nudges! Honest.

## Speak to clients, not peers

Comparisonitis has a lot to answer for when it comes to the way you show up. It often leads to mimicking, aka being less you and more them. This leaves you open to the risk of sharing things in a way you hope will impress your industry peers. Often this looks like what I like to call the 'faux-enthusiasm effect': being suddenly overcome with a massive gush of excitement for the thing you're selling because that's what you think you need to do, because it's what all your peers seem to be doing and you want to fit in. *I am so excited to announce that doors to my new course are open!* Here's why this is problematic.

1.   Are you *really* this excited though?
2.   Does this accord with your natural personality? If not, pretending is going to give off more than a subtle whiff of pretence, which let's face it, isn't the sales vibe anyone wants to lead with.
3.   What incentive are you giving your client to buy with this ridiculously unspecific expression of excitement?

To be clear: your followers don't wake up in the morning wishing for you to be more like someone you're not and they certainly, absolutely, 100% do not buy things purely because you expressed excitement for them.

The *only* person you should be thinking about when you're creating content or showing up online is your lovely client. Not other people in your industry or niche, not the mates who watch all your Stories.

When you focus on your clients (the people who actually want to buy from you) and not your peers, you'll find it much easier to know what to say and how to say it in your own voice. They care about how you solve their problem, so sack off feeling like you've got to get your jazz hands out and tell them that instead!

## Know your people well

People buy things they want to have. So, what do your people want?

Showing up and promoting your products means advocating for the things you know your clients want, by connecting what you're selling with their desires. Buying decisions are led by desire, so your job as the salesperson is to speak to what people want and create connection to what you're selling by making it clear how what you're offering is relevant to that particular desire. Why should they care about your product?

If I don't want to buy what you're selling, if I don't see it as relevant for what I want right now, it doesn't matter how good you are at sales, I'm just not going to buy it.

## Stop taking it so personally

Promoting your business or products once and then getting annoyed when you don't get flooded with orders straight away is a bit like rocking up for your first day at school and being upset you didn't get picked for prefect by lunch. People don't buy on the first go – and you shouldn't want them to! If they did that, they'd be doing it without giving due thought or attention to what you're actually selling, which can't possibly be painted out in glorious technicolour in the first post. It takes *time* for people to get to know your products, and even when they do know them, not all buyers in your audience will be ready for what you're selling at the exact moment you're selling it.

In the beginning, it feels so personal when you put yourself out there and nobody buys your stuff. I mean how can it not when it's *your* work and *you* are the one doing the selling, right?

Rejection is a bitter pill to swallow – sure – I mean just ask anyone who's got down on one knee to propose, and been told no. It stings. The good news is, unlike marriage proposals, a no isn't personal and it's actually a good thing. I mean think about it: if every single person you put yourself out there in front of bought from you there's no *way* they'd all be perfect clients. So then you'd be open to complaints, unsatisfying outcomes, and goodness knows what else. That is not how we like to roll. Round here we *like* people to pull up their big girl pants and *tell us* when they don't want to work with us. People don't buy things to be polite, and why on earth would we want them to?

So if someone said no it means (a) the timing isn't right for them or (b) they don't want what you're selling. Not personal. Not a big deal. Just a happy outcome all round.

It's almost time to get out there and take action! Go on, admit it, you're chomping at the bit after that little pep talk. I can totally tell.

## Taking action: your energy always leads

Sales are driven by exchanging energy with your audience. Without sales, you will have no business – it really is that simple! People won't buy what they can't see, don't understand or didn't know existed, and so the energy exchange starts with you showing up and getting the ball rolling.

The better we can become at communicating with our audience, talking about how we help and why people work with us, the easier we make it for people to say yes to buying. Showing up is how we ensure a high standard of care, personalized support and clients getting the results they are looking for.

The goal is to make this regular contribution to helping your audience understand what it is that you do and why, so that they can buy with confidence, in a way that feels energizing, natural and automatic.

## The compound effect of visibility

As we saw in Chapter 9, selling on social media is about sharing regular messages with your audience in a way that's easy for them to digest. It's not about trends or becoming a designer or an expert in creating fancy video transitions, it's an opportunity for you to connect with your audience in a medium that suits you, whether that medium be the written word, pictures, or video. We are lucky we have a choice, but let's not confuse the plethora of options with 'must do it all' because it's not the case. It's far more important to do less, but do it often.

We are not able to predict exactly when our clients will be online, nor do we need to try. What we do need to do is ensure a rhythm to the content we create, so that on any given day, when someone in your audience comes online they are met with a piece of content that's relevant for their stage of the buyer journey. This is why it's so important to take sales action every day, and to do it in minutes and have it be no big deal.

I want to spend a moment talking about consistency here: not because it's a *s e x y* word because I think we can all agree it's really not, in fact so much so that I'm actually going to swap it out right now for *regularity* instead, which is better, albeit marginally.

Waiting to feel excited to take action and then being disappointed when the sales don't come flooding in is like turning up to only half your classes and then wondering why you didn't get top marks. Without regularity, the impact of your content, your visibility effort is severely limited to that one action in isolation. But that's not what your content is meant for. It's meant to be a rolling constant that delivers relevant snippets. The effect on your audience on the days when you aren't present, is that they lose interest, de-prioritize the decision they were halfway through making, or forget about you altogether. And that results in your sales activity falling on deaf ears, because not enough people in your audience are warm enough to be ready to buy it.

Regularity bonds your activity together to much greater effect. With social media, it's never about creating a long form masterpiece, it's about greeting your audience where they are, with snippets of information that, over time, add up to a compelling amount of connection and confidence in you. It's like saying good morning to your colleague at the coffee machine each morning – not chewing her ear off for 25 minutes every day while she's trying to grab her flat white. Over time, that small, repeatable action you take snowballs into a huge, compounded boulder of warming, nourishing goodwill in your business. The momentum that is created from the simple commitment to share simple messages that help your audience over and over again is worth more to you than any one piece of isolated content can.

## Stopping the stop start: finding momentum (and keeping it)

Momentum carries your business forward even in busy periods or when motivation wanes. Having clarity on what needs to happen to bring in sales 'no matter what' protects you from having to start from scratch every time you want to sell something.

Every day, your audience will be made up of people at the colder end of the journey, and people who are much warmer and closer to buying. No matter the split, each stage requires your active participation to keep the nurturing process in motion. We can improve our level of client focus by showing up with a baseline level of visibility, that doesn't require our maximum energy level, and can still get done even on the days when our energy is elsewhere.

Focusing on how to create momentum in your sales means keeping a steady flow of new business, so that you don't have to start from scratch (aka the cold end of the nurturing process) every time you want to sign new clients. When your non-negotiables are clear and set ahead of time, it's much easier for your business to stay in momentum, even on the days when natural motivation levels are fluctuating or life gets in the way.

We can maintain momentum by having a minimum set of committed actions that keep sales coming in no matter what. There's a big difference between what *needs* to get done and what's nice to get done, and knowing what this looks like keeps your business moving forwards even on the days when time is short. Revisit the needle movers from Chapter 4 if you need a refresh.

If we can show up on more days than not, in a way that feels light and doesn't take more than a few minutes, we not only keep client focus, but we also free ourselves from the idea that showing up has to depend on whether you feel inspired or motivated to do so. In reality, the two are not linked, nor should they be. A sustainable business makes money day in, day out – not just on the days when your personal energy levels are high.

We all love the days when you feel endless excitement for what you're creating and the opportunities available to you. On these days, motivation levels are through the roof – natural magnetism is coursing through your veins, and you feel invincible. Getting visible is a breeze when you feel like this, after all – you can do anything! Show up and talk on the internet? Sure! So much to say! So much to share! Ideas for days!

Motivation is not a constant resource. On some days, there's an abundance of it, but on others – well – it's just not as high as you might like. That doesn't make you a bad business owner, it makes you human.

Then, there are the days where nothing is going right, you want to burn the whole thing down and climb under a rock. The days when your bank account is precariously low, you have emails coming out of your ears, there are people wanting things from you everywhere you look, nothing seems to be going right, the to-do list is out of control, and you find yourself wondering why on earth you gave up a regular pay cheque to work this hard and feel this broke. Maybe it's the school holidays, maybe there are other contributing factors to why you feel so wrung out.

On days like this, the last thing you feel like doing is showing up on the blooming internet and putting yourself out there for the world to see, judge and critique. Allowing your business to fail because your motivation did a runner isn't going to help your clients, it won't help you and it doesn't make the world a better place. What *will* benefit everyone, though, is more people growing businesses that are thriving. Your business surviving is part of something huge, and keeping it quiet, charging too little or giving up entirely simply won't do. This plan is for those days. Showing up with a minimum level of visibility that keeps more of your audience warm is one of the most powerful things you can do for your sales and your business. When you do this, you build familiarity and trust over time. You speed up the nurturing process and you facilitate confident action taking. This is not something to rush in one fell swoop. Understanding that the point of social media is to be a routine hello rather than a one-time pitch is one of the biggest time savers I can give you.

## The 30-day sales challenge

It's time to get laser focused on your sales activities for 30 days so you can build the momentum that feeds your business and sell with confidence, in just a few minutes each day!

To make it as simple as possible for you to stay the course, here you'll find 30 days of prompts that you can use over and over again. Use it to get started, to draw inspiration from or to re-start after a break and get back into action.

To help you get visible and consistent with your selling, challenge yourself to show up and sell every day – *yes*, every day for 30 days! Boost your confidence on social media, connect with more clients and increase your sales without having to do any of the thinking. The intention for the next 30 days is that you are able to show up with clarity and consistency to share information about your business that will help your audience get to know your products and services.

These prompts have been designed to provide a foundation of nurturing for buyers at every stage of the journey (cold, warm and hot). When used in isolation they will provide a solid benchmark of content for social media. I recommend that you cycle through these prompts at least once so that you can start building your momentum. Then, once it has become second nature to you to share sales messages in this way, you can expand your sales activities or build out your action from there.

All you have to do is pick one of the prompts below (choosing from a different category each day) and share a piece of content created around that prompt. Use this as your starting point and your daily minimum and notice how quickly traction builds! Small, repeatable daily actions are all you need.

## For your cold audience: Connection content

As we learned in Chapter 9, connection content is how you greet new people into your world. It helps the colder end of your audience, who don't know you yet, find those initial threads of curiosity that will capture their imagination and make them want to find out more. Connection content incorporates stories and personal brand elements that draw people into your world, as well as giving evidence of the type of information you share on your topic.

Connection content is also important for introducing the theme your service helps with – so they can identify that your offers are for them, and you are someone they want to be following and paying attention to.

This is where you create the content that connects the wants of your clients with the solutions you're offering, demonstrating understanding of their aspirations and building know, like and trust by sharing personal stories.

### Ten prompts to help build connection
1. Introduce yourself.
2. Share why your business exists and why people come to you.
3. Talk about a personal experience you've had that made you want to make the industry better (can be good or bad).

4.  Share a statistic which brings relevance to the topic you're talking about.
5.  Create intrigue for your product by alluding to the main applications.
6.  Share some key elements from your own story to illustrate similarities between you and your client – to show that you've been where they are now, and/or worked with lots of people who are where they are right now.
7.  Think of your ideal client's pain points and address one of those pain points in a post. For example, three tools for overcoming X, five ways to achieve X, how I managed to stop [audience challenge or struggle].
8.  On the flip side, think of your ideal client's aspirations/goals/wants and needs and address one of those in a reel. For example, Want to [client aspiration], try this; Here's how I [achieved client goal]; Three steps to [getting what your client wants].
9.  Talk about a common struggle you work through with your clients and describe that pain point in detail – to help your audience self-identify that you're the right fit for them.
10. Share a case study of a client from the pain points and struggles they were experiencing before working with you (so your ideal client can identify themselves in that pain point too) to how they felt after working with you.

## For your warm audience: confidence content

Confidence content warms your audience up further by deepening connection. Confidence content shares what you're thinking and doing, together with lessons, experiences, things you've learned and your beliefs. It's also an opportunity to combine your views and share bite-sized teaching moments or education around your topic.

### Ten prompts to help build confidence

1. Tell your audience what they can expect from working with you.
2. What is the most common mistake you see people doing?
3. When you see people being stuck, what in your opinion is the most common reason why?
4. How do you simplify things for your clients?
5. When is the right time to consider working with someone like you?
6. Who are you for/not for?
7. What is missing from your industry that you wish there was more of?
8. Share the result that you're intending for people.
9. What gets you fired up to do this work?
10. What are your beliefs about your subject matter?

## For your hot audience: conviction content

This is the type of content that allows your audience to get to know their options, and activates them to make a decision. Without this type of content in your strategy, you'll create a legion of loyal followers who don't necessarily convert to sales (because you didn't ask them to). The goal with conviction content is to allow people to feel sure in their decision making.

### Ten prompts to help build conviction

1. Describe who your products and services are for. You could start with 'My [offer] is for you if... [describe the pain points your ideal audience have]' *and* describe who your offer is *not* for: 'This isn't for you if... [describe the people it's not a good fit for]'. This will help you call in action takers.
2. Explain how your offer works, describe the start and end points and how they transition from A to B. Talk about how it works and how they will feel at each step in the journey.

3. Describe the transition and result of working with you. 'After working with me you will be able to... '
4. Share a testimonial or a case study that shows how you helped a client go from your ideal client's pain point, through the transition process (describe what that looked like), to the final result – to demonstrate the transformation you can create for them too.
5. Share social proof – a screen grab of a message from a happy client, or better still jump on a livestream video chat with a happy client to discuss their transition from [pain point] to [client goal].
6. Detail how working with you will feel, what the process looks like from sign up to the process to completing, and describe what you will do to support them along the way.
7. Make it ridiculously clear what people will (and will not) get from working with you.
8. Include the tangible benefits (for example, calls/email support/a community) and the intangible benefits (for example, feeling supported/getting a confidence boost/ overcoming self-sabotage).
9. Describe how your audience will know when it's the right time to sign up so they can self-identify whether it's the right time for them to click 'buy now!'
10. Speak to the possible objections your ideal clients are facing – are they worried they won't get the same results as your other clients; do they feel like they 'don't have the time' for your course/service or are they worried about the investment? Share content that will help them overcome these worries and make a confident decision about working with you.

Make it easier still: Play Sales Bingo!

You can find my 30-day cheat sheet along with the other resources that accompany this book, here: www.saradalrymple. co.uk/moresalesplease

# When it's working: selling in direct messages

When your social media activity is doing its job, you'll know about it because you'll start getting more enquiries and sales!

In Chapter 7, we talked about sales conversations and how to lead them with integrity. The same is true when the conversation is happening via social media, only this time, it might not be an actual conversation, it might all happen right there in the platform via personal or direct messages. When a potential client reaches out via personal message or direct message, it is another opportunity to blow their socks off with your incredible service and help them with their decision about whether to work with you. So, how can you give off friendly and approachable vibes, without getting friend-zoned? Here are my top tips for how to approach selling in this way:

- *Have confidence.* It's very rare that someone will just buy from you without messaging you first. So, when someone reaches out to you for information, be sure to have confidence and clarity in the process you are using. Remember that this is your specialist topic, so lead with the value it delivers. Your role is to discover what your client wants, and then to advocate for what you know can help them.
- *Seek clarity.* Start by asking relevant questions. You might start by saying something along the lines of: 'Thanks so much for getting in touch – I'd love to hear more about what's happening for you!' Open the conversation loop so that your client can then tell you what they are experiencing and their desire from here.
- *Get to the root of the problem by asking questions.* First you must discover what the problem is, then from there you can establish whether you have the right solution for that problem, and signpost from there. Before you can provide a solution with integrity, you must

understand the full scope of the situation. Continue asking questions until you understand what is needed and what solution might help. Ask your client what they believe to be the reason why they haven't been able to get results. And then ask yourself, can I help them with this?

- *Ask yourself if you can help.* Use boatloads of your own discernment here. This person is relying on you to provide your honest view on whether you can help, and if it's not a good fit, signpost them on. Once you have established suitability and know where they want to go, invite them to find out more about how you can help.

- *Client care.* Deliver on what you promised. Showing up, doing what you said you'd do. Get results, deliver the dream. The goal is to have happy clients (products) or get results (service) so you have raving fans who then recommend you to others. Then your content, your questions and your raving fans do the selling for you.

Sell every day. The magic of social media is in using it to deliver small, bite-sized snippets of information that take minutes to deliver and help your clients make decisions. Do that every day and watch your sales explode!

## Tamu Thomas on ... finding your ease with self-promotion

Tamu Thomas is an emotional well-being coach trained in somatic coaching, with a background in social work. She is a writer, workshop facilitator, podcaster and Non-Linear Movement practitioner.

'When I first started selling I felt very self-conscious, I felt like I was asking people for their money rather than their money being exchanged for a valuable service. I also had a strong belief that making comfortable money was *hard*, so I found making money from something I enjoy really challenging. This would show up as not sending invoices for ages, undercharging and over-working and not keeping track of my finances. My income was like a rollercoaster with medium highs and plummeting lows. I was totally in an abusive relation-ship with sales (and money)!

Now I know that selling allows me to do my job and that pricing with integrity helps sales feel like I'm joyfully campaigning as I believe in myself, what I do and the impact it has. I have chosen to make the way I work fun. I create products and services in a manner that is friendly for my nervous system, not easy but easeful. As well as giving me a sense of pride it's healed some of my 'money is hard' patterning.

This shift has transformed my energy around selling: I am now galvanized and compelled by what I do so it's easy to advocate for it. I'm not talking about perfec-tion, but I am so certain about what I offer I can share it powerfully. Becoming compelled by my offer instead of just following a formula helped me to create services and events I can fully back.

The impact of finding ease with self-promotion is simple: sustainable income. I am so proud that I make my own money and that this money I create with my heart, brain, gut and laptop looks after my daughter and me. And I do this on 21 hours a week, taking naps, having baths at 3pm and enjoying my local park before the school children get there, chef's kiss! Selling with more ease means that I have prospective clients approaching me. I've been booked for cool corporate gigs and been approached by a book publisher.'

## Tamu's top tips

Look at what you are selling and ask yourself if you're proud of it, not if it's perfect, but are you proud? Joy in promoting and selling your work starts on the inside. It's essential to separate your innate unquestionable worth and value from the value of your work. When you are clear about this, mistakes and missteps in business remain about business rather than a character flaw. This way you can adapt, pivot, apologize or stop with more grace. I see too many people make their business success about their personal worth. This makes business owners act like influencers rather than entrepreneurs.

Small repeatable actions I prioritize include showing up, promoting and selling – it makes you visible. Marketing, promotion and sales take about 60% of my time. Over time, your messaging gets clearer and more refined which builds your credibility, expertise and thought leadership. I do a regular vibe check about my services. If the vibe is off, I look at what is needed and make changes or end it. *Boundaries!!!* I cannot stress this enough. You need to have clear boundaries for yourself, especially when you work with other humans. Repurpose your content and, no matter what you think, you are not selling too much!

I met Tamu in a Mastermind a few years ago and haven't stopped smiling since. She is joy personified. Find her at @livethreesixty on Instagram or her website www.livethreesixty.com/ and thank me later.

# Now it's your turn!

## To sell every day

Introduce self-promotion into your daily routine. Take the 30-day challenge to set the wheels in motion! Before you begin:

- Do you have a bank of up-to-date photos of yourself you actually like? It's not essential but it is so much easier to show up on busy days or when inspiration is waning if you have a file full of images you can use alongside your message of the day.
- Set aside 30 minutes each day to complete your promotion activity.
- Keep it simple. This is not about getting it perfect, it's about getting into the swing of taking daily action.

Remember: this doesn't need to take more than a few minutes a day – in fact, it's not supposed to take longer than a few minutes each day! The goal is, small, repeatable actions that create clarity and compound over time.

# Chapter recap

If you take one thing away from this chapter let it be this: doing sales activity on social media daily will shrink the timeframe on how long it takes people to make decisions and will skyrocket your sales.

- The magic of social media is in using it to deliver regular messages that help your audience make confident decisions that are right for them. The better you can be at using social media to support your sales plan the more sales you will make.
- The value is in the compounding: no one post is going to create sales on its own, but the momentum you create over time keeps your audience warm, and this is the place sales decisions are made from.

- Single action is not the goal, it's about contributing snippets of clarity regularly so that your audience stays warm.
- Don't wait for inspiration to strike – set a routine and stick to that. You'll be so glad you did.

This chapter gives you a starting point for what I hope will be a long lasting, effective and easeful relationship between you and social media. The more business owners we can get promoting their products in this way and being seen by ideal clients, the more of an economic impact we can create!

# Summary

There's a saying in the small business community that goes something along the lines of 'Every time you buy from a small business owner, they do a little happy dance'. I love a happy dance, and if it's to a nineties tune, even better!

Hearing your phone or computer 'ping' with a sale coming through never fails to raise a smile. Getting paid for work you love to create, by people who value the way you do what you do is a whole vibe and it just never gets old. But that ping of a sale is about so much more than dancing. Financial independence, effecting change, growing the economy without selling your soul... the list goes on and on. The small business community is such an important part of the UK economy and the more it thrives, the better for everyone!

You now have the foundation, the method and the prompts to equip you to do your daily promotional activity with confidence. Chapter by chapter, we have explored how to increase your sales in less time so that you can grow without the grind.

Far from the general perception that it's 'hard' to make money or to sell well, making lots and lots of sales for your business gets to be easy when you have a plan that's aligned for you. Now that you've read this book, you have everything you need to do just that and to do it in a way that fits into your daily life in just a few minutes. Through repeatable action you can start, and keep going, even when life gets in the way, without having to rely on inspiration, motivation or luck.

I truly believe that sales skills are the best gift you can give your business. They allow you to sustain your business, make money on your own terms and do work you love for as long as you want to..

Einstein said 'Life is like riding a bicycle. To keep your balance, you must keep moving.' The same is true with sales.

Your 30-day challenge awaits, and the more you do it, the better your results will be. Eventually, promoting your products will be so natural you won't need the prompts any more, but until then, use them as much as you need.

SMEs already contribute more than half of private sector turnover in the UK, and that's without 60% of them harnessing the power of confident promotion online. Half of business owners polled by OnePoll feel they could have made more sales if they had marketed themselves properly online.

Imagine the additional revenue, the jobs and the impact that would be generated from people doing what they love and talking about it more regularly on the internet. As I always say, if all of the business owners using social media spent just a few minutes each day promoting and selling their products, the amount of income created would be mind blowing.

Let's blow some minds and do some happy dances, shall we?

Sara x

# Get in touch

If you have enjoyed reading *More Sales Please* I would love it if you could leave me a review on Amazon and recommend it to your business owner communities. Reviews make such a difference and help other potential readers get a good idea of why to buy the book. Your support means the absolute world to me. Thank you!

I miss colleagues! It's been years since I had a water cooler moment, a chat by the coffee machine or a natter with a new joiner in the break out area. So don't be a stranger – say hello, tell me how you're getting on! I love talking about sales and helping business owners increase theirs, so come and chat to me any time. You can find me on Instagram @saleswithsara.

I love helping people find their ease with selling, so if you'd like me to run a training session for your community, get in touch. If you would like more personalized support, you can find out about my sales training programmes and ongoing mentorship options here: www.saradalrymple.co.uk.

And don't forget, all resources that accompany this book can be found here: www.saradalrymple.co.uk/more salesplease

# Glossary

**Authentic:** If something is authentic, it is real, true or what people say it is.

**Burnout:** The WHO defines burnout as a syndrome caused by uncontrolled chronic stress in the workplace. People with this syndrome will have the following characteristics: feeling drained of energy or exhausted, feeling increasingly distant mentally – that is, feeling negative, cynical – from the job they are doing and finally a decrease in professional efficiency.

**Buyer journey:** The customer's path to purchase. During this process potential clients build awareness of what they desire and the options available to them, and then make a decision.

**Communication strategy:** What you're saying (your message, content and communication/sales skills). This is how you attract your clients and get your work into the hands of the people who want it. It matters just as much as the product or service itself, because if you can't capture the attention and imagination of your audience, nobody will buy it.

**Evergreen/sustainable marketing:** content that nurtures your home on the internet, aka your website. Evergreen marketing centres around attracting people over to your website where you can nurture them with blog content and invite them to buy from you. This is in contrast to using social media content, which technically you don't have ownership of.

**Lead generation:** The activity you take to create sales conversations. A large part of lead generation comes via the content you create, but it also includes the places you are visible, the messaging on your website and your promotional activity.

**Marketing:** One part of the sales process: it's everything you do to attract the right clients into your world. This might be the copy on your website, what you say at networking events, the content you put onto social media, the things you say on your blog, the emails you send, the podcast episodes you create, etc. If its goal is to call in the right clients, it's marketing.

**Messaging:** Your messaging allows you to confidently attract clients, establish your voice, build authority in your space. It's how your clients get to know you, it's what leads to enquiries, decisions, sales and long lasting, happy relationships. Its role is to hook your audience in by clearly letting them know you can help them. Done right, it attracts clients, allows them to move through the buyer journey and opt in to your service and speeds up the sales process. If your messaging is too vague, your client will lose interest before wanting to buy from you.

**Offer strategy:** What you're selling (offer creation and packaging). Before you can sell anything, you need to be clear about *what* you're selling and *why*. Offer strategy means packaging up your knowledge or skills into a product or service that is desirable for the people you want to buy it. This is where you make sure you are creating something people will actually buy. Its role is to make sure your service is specific enough to speak to a certain group of potential clients, the value to those people is clearly articulated, and a change is delivered. Setting your offers up in this way does the hard work so your audience doesn't have to. Nail it by defining a clear niche, articulating the value, being sure about the change you're enabling.

**Offers:** The range of products and services you sell in your business.

**Personal brand:** The stories and narrative you provide that share the more human side of your business. Your sales superpower!

**Promotion activity:** the range of actions you take to market and sell your products to clients. In other words, how you talk about what you do, where you do so and how often.

**Sales process:** The journey you go on *with* your client before they decide whether to buy from you or not. This comprises marketing and sales activities that, together, help your audience get to know you, what you have available for them to buy, and the wider context within which your business sits.

**Sales strategy:** The set of actions you take in your business to attract new clients, establish suitability and provide the information they need to make informed choices. The thing that ring fences your time and moves people from cold leads to warmed up and ready to buy/not buy; in any case make a decision about whether to work with you.

**Visibility strategy:** Where you're saying it (where you find new clients) in real life versus online visibility, or perhaps a combination of both. If you're going to be on social media, do so as part of your sales strategy instead of at random. This ensures that when you show up, you do so in an intentional way that's timely and gets results.

# A handy list of sales activities for when inspiration has dried up

Here are my top lead-generating sales activities – handy for when there's no time to think. Just pick one and go!

1. Create a social media post or email telling people how they can work with you or buy from you in the next month and send it out: today.
2. Get visible with your existing audience social media, and include a specific call to action at the end. Why not challenge yourself to talk to camera and tell your audience one thing that inspired you to set up your business?
3. Share a recent testimonial or case study explaining where your client started, why they came to work with you, and how it ended. It really helps people visualize what's possible for them!
4. Introduce yourself and remind your audience how they can work with you or what your products do for them. Do this at least once a week.
5. Ask recent clients or purchasers for feedback and share it with your community when it comes in.
6. Check in with past clients to follow up on how their progress is going and see if they'd like to buy a top-up at a special price.
7. Think about the results you're best at delivering for people, and share them with your audience.
8. Host a flash sale for a limited time and combine it with a reminder of what each product in the sale does for the client you intended it for.
9. Remind your audience who you *are* for and who you are *not* for.

10. Offer a referral fee for past clients who recommend you to their communities.

11. Create a piece of content that explains the number one thing you know how to fix for your audience. Pin it somewhere that your audience can find it again and again.

12. Respond to all comments and messages you receive on social media – it's not a one-way street, have conversations!

13. Make contact with the hosts of three podcasts you'd like to be featured on, explaining why you're such a good fit for their podcast audience.

14. Go to a new networking event either in real life or online, and practise using your who what why statement telling people what you do *for them*!

15. Create a fun resource on something really valuable for the people you want to work with and make it available for free on your website in exchange for signing up to your email list.

# Troubleshooting:
# Help – where are my sales?

There are a multitude of potential reasons why something isn't selling yet. It could be to do with time, the energetics behind the way you're selling it, or the clarity. It could also be that you just haven't been selling for long enough yet. Don't lose heart. Here's a handy list of places to start looking for answers.

## Belief

Is it immediately obvious to anyone who comes across your profile what exactly it is you're delivering? If this is in any way woolly, your audience will have a hard time believing in your product enough to buy it. They need:

- belief in you as an expert and authority in your subject area;
- belief in you and your product to deliver on its promise;
- belief in their ability to get the result you're promoting.

## Audience

Are you focusing on growing an audience of people who want this exact thing? If you don't have a large enough number of the right people, you have an audience problem.

- Who's your who? Can they self-identify easily?
- Is the relevance and value clear?
- What does your audience *want*? What's driving their desire for change?

## Strategy

Is the content you're producing getting in front of new people *and* helping your existing audience warm up to making a decision? If this is messy or incomplete, tighten up your strategy.

- Do you have a process that positions what you know?
- Are you visible in the right places and regularly?
- How are you piquing interest and getting people's attention?
- Are you using the wrong strategy for your personality?
- Are you using any strategy at all?

## Experience

Are you delivering a buying experience that is 'just OK' or are you leading your clients through the most enjoyable, light and easy process they've ever come across?

- Is the customer experience easy to follow at all stages?
- Are you serving your audience to the best of your ability?
- Is it easy to find the right information and to take next steps?
- Do you provide answers to questions and provide support at every part of the decision-making process, or are you leaving them to figure it out alone?
- How can you make it a dream for them?

# Acknowledgements

I thought it might be really isolating for someone like me, who gets her energy from being around people, to write a book. And don't get me wrong, I've put my hours in at the keyboard. But, this hasn't been something I've done alone – far from it – it's been a real collaboration from start to finish and that has been right up my street. The support of others and the community around me that have helped make this book a reality has been everything.

I don't think I'll ever be able to go into a bookshop again without an overwhelming sense of the amount of work that has gone into every title, and the number of people who helped make each one happen.

Here are some of mine – it simply wouldn't have happened without you all, thank you!

To Alison Jones at Practical Inspiration Publishing, for choosing my book as the winner of the September 2022 book proposal challenge, and to Lee Griffith for encouraging me to enter in the first place. I do love our co-working days, what on earth are you going to make me do next?

To all the fabulous business owners who contributed their expertise and inspiring stories so generously: Lara Sheldrake, Helen Perry, Louisa Clarke, Lou Chudley, Helen Bamborough, Ami Roberson, Vicki Knights, Lucie Sheridan, Lucy Werner, Josephine Brooks and Tamu Thomas.

To Erin Chamberlain and Steph Caswell – my fabulous book coach friends who gave me so much guidance and support on this journey.

To my beta readers Jane Galloway, Kendall Platt, Emily Armitage, Nikki Edwards, Helen Pretty and Sarah Holstead for your valuable feedback and comments which were so very appreciated.

To fellow authors Lucy Werner, Katie Tucker and Catherine Erdly for answering questions about the process and helping me keep my head on straight!

To my mentoring clients, my course participants and my community for bringing your passion and fantastic ideas into our work and for allowing me to help you turn them into sustainable revenue streams for your business. I love supporting you, I love the questions you ask, I love the fun we have and, most of all, I love showing you how to build your financial power.

To my family:

Dave – thank you for letting me hide away in my office for weekends on end to get this book written while you ran around town taking the boys to everything from birthday parties to sports fixtures, never once complaining. And on top of that, for every extra hour you found so that I could stay in the 'zone' a tiny bit longer. We're a good team, you and me.

Hannah – the best sister there is. I'm so grateful to you for everything. Couldn't do it without you, and that's that.

Mum, Dad – thank you for coming round and keeping us in delicious home cooked food so that I could plough on without stopping to keep my hungry brood fed and watered. 'Go for it' and 'never give up': the two mantras I got from you that made this happen.

Joe and Max – my lovely boys, you inspire me every day. You are funny, brave, endlessly encouraging and kind. I couldn't ask for anything more. Family is everything and if I can teach you one thing let it be this: believe in yourself because when you do, anything is possible.

To all my friends who always know what to say, but especially to Jen, Andrea, Jane and Kerry for being the best cheerleaders a girl could wish for; to Katie for coming with me on my writer's retreat, giving me pep talks every morning and taking me to the most incredible hotel for dinner to celebrate; and to

Charlotte, Cara and Holly for making me howl with laughter over a glass or three. Friends are just the best, aren't they?

Finally, to my 12-year-old self who taught herself to touch type during lunch breaks in the school computer room for no apparent reason. It all finally makes sense.

# Index

# A quick word from Practical Inspiration Publishing...

We hope you found this book both practical and inspiring – that's what we aim for with every book we publish.

We publish titles on topics ranging from leadership, entrepreneurship, HR and marketing to self-development and wellbeing.

Find details of all our books at: www.practicalinspiration.com

 **Did you know...**

We can offer discounts on bulk sales of all our titles – ideal if you want to use them for training purposes, corporate giveaways or simply because you feel these ideas deserve to be shared with your network.

We can even produce bespoke versions of our books, for example with your organization's logo and/or a tailored foreword.

To discuss further, contact us on info@practicalinspiration.com.

 **Got an idea for a business book?**

We may be able to help. Find out more about publishing in partnership with us at: bit.ly/PIpublishing.

*Follow us on social media...*

@PIPTalking

@pip_talking

@practicalinspiration

@piptalking

Practical Inspiration Publishing

9 781788 604659